THE

LUXURY

COLLECTION®

GLOBAL ARTISANS

Content © 2018 Marriott International
Design © 2018 Assouline Publishing
3 Park Avenue, 27th Floor
New York, NY 10016, USA
Tel: 212-989-6769 Fax: 212-647-0005
www.assouline.com
ISBN: 9781614286813
Printed in China
Color separation by Artron Printing
Editorial direction: Esther Kremer
Art direction: Jihyun Kim & Charlotte Sivrière
Editor: Lindsey Tulloch

THE
LUXURY
COLLECTION®

GLOBAL ARTISANS

ASSOULINE

CONTENTS

LATIN AMERICA

NORTH AMERICA

CURATING THE PERFECT STAY

By Whitney Robinson

I've never been the kind of traveler who randomly picks his next destination. I don't stand in front of a map, Google or otherwise, and throw proverbial darts, nor do I choose where to go based on any particular activities (though I'm still pretty adventurous) or geography (though I've never met a beach I didn't love). I'm not even the kind of guy who travels based on the weather—sun or snow are but minor details in my selection process. Rather, I choose a destination based on one simple criterion: Whether it's twenty-four hours in Milan or a month in Marrakech, for me, it's all about the hotel. A hotel is much more than just a place to stay after a day of exploring or a practical pit stop on the way to another destination. For a self-professed hotel aficionado like me, the hotel is the destination. Hotels represent everything I love about travel: the discovery, the history, the architecture, the food, the music, and the design of a place. In cities, they function as living rooms (especially in my hometown of Manhattan, where squeezing in ten friends for dinner can be a challenge). And in some cases, as with the hotels that make up The Luxury Collection, they can be even more iconic than the locations themselves.

Take, for example, one of my favorite hotels in the world: The Gritti Palace. The Gritti isn't just another palazzo in Venice—it *is* Venice, from the Fortuny-covered walls to the custom Riva

Hand-colored artwork on cloth in Jaipur, India.

speedboat parked outside, ready to ferry lucky guests to the glassmaking ateliers in Murano or to bask in the sun on the Lido. I have spent many days sitting on that famous floating dock with a plate of *spaghetti frutti di mare* handmade by Chef Daniele Turco or drinking a Bellini by moonlight and looking out at the magnificent Santa Maria della Salute church, thinking: *Who would ever want to leave?*

It's much the same in Athens, where my favorite afternoon custom is to drink ouzo on the rocks at the rooftop bar of the Hotel Grande Bretagne, watching the sun set over the Parthenon. In Paris, I have admired the intricate wrought-iron beauty of a courtyard at the Prince de Galles. In Sardinia on the Costa Smeralda, it was the terrazzo floors at the Hotel Pitrizza. In Milan, at the Excelsior Hotel Gallia, I have marveled at the brutalist Milanese train station outside my suite window. And I fell for Lake Geneva at Hotel President Wilson. If the twentieth century was about the acquisition of material goods and the twenty-first is about experiences, there have been no better memory-makers than these.

In other words, for me, the best and most memorable hotel stay should do three things: It should educate you about your local environs, it should motivate you to live your life differently, and it should definitely make you smile. This latest book in The Luxury Collection's series, published by Assouline, is dedicated to the authenticity that comes along with a stay at a hotel that mindfully includes locally crafted elements within its guest experience. Each of these Luxury Collection destinations has graciously shared how it brings the spirit of the surrounding area into the property. In these pages, you'll read about the meticulously embroidered uniforms worn by the staff of Al Manara in Jordan; the handcrafted lauhala bracelets at The Royal Hawaiian in Waikiki on Honolulu; the Olinalá lacquerware trays used at Las Alcobas in Mexico City to deliver items to guests; the bespoke silk wall panel gracing the lobby of The Azure Qiantang in Hangzhou, China; the onsite coral nursery that transplants and rehabilitates damaged corals at The Andaman in Malaysia; and so many more colorful and fascinating stories. The result is an inspiring book of suggestions for the best starting points in the world from which to choose your next adventure.

Chandelier and Nymph of the Danube sculpture at Hotel Imperial, Vienna, Austria.

STORY OF
THE LUXURY COLLECTION

The Luxury Collection is an ensemble of more than one hundred of the world's finest hotels and resorts, each noteworthy for its architecture, art, furniture, amenities, cuisine, and distinctive heritage. Our properties all share the goal of offering guests authentic experiences that are inextricably linked to each destination, and the skills of dedicated artisans add the finishing touches to an unparalleled stay at every one.

Within a world of hotels spanning five continents and countless cultural influences, The Luxury Collection celebrates an astounding diversity of craftsmanship. In this volume, *The Luxury Collection: Global Artisans*, we introduce the artists and artisans whose original work and careful attention to detail make each property unique, exploring these artfully crafted aspects of our hotels in vivid detail.

Imagine yourself admiring the Murano stained-glass panels, made by a master Venetian glassblower, at Hotel Danieli's Palazzo Dandolo; relaxing in a handcrafted Yucatecan hammock at Hacienda Puerta Campeche; tasting real maple syrup at The Equinox from the trees on Vermont's Dutton Farm; enjoying the melodious sound produced by a guitar from Álvarez & Bernal near Hotel Alfonso XIII; or marveling at The Athenee Hotel's impressive collection of intricate Thai silk embroidery. Artisanal featuresare carefully curated to delight guests' senses, offering artwork, products, and experiences of the highest quality.

From an intricate brass-adorned dowry chest in each guest room at Al Maha in Dubai, to a traditional Austrian dirndl customized with Swarovski crystals and Hotel Goldener Hirsch's colors in Salzburg, to a line of spa products made from lavender indigenous to the Carolinas at The Ballantyne, the hotels' artisanal elements are bound to dazzle and charm. The artists and craftspeople who partner with The Luxury Collection put their hearts into everything they create, and we hope their work is an inspiration to all.

AFRICA & THE MIDDLE EAST

AL MAHA

DUBAI, UNITED ARAB EMIRATES

A BRIDE'S MOST PRIZED POSSESSION

There are said to be three furnishings in an Omani house: the doors, the windows, and a dowry chest, or *mandoos*. Specific types of chests are named with reference to a place—Omani, Kuwaiti, Bahraini, Zanzibari, for example—but this often designates where the piece was acquired or used rather than where it was made. For centuries and across many countries, when women wed, it was customary for them to bring a dowry chest filled with money, linens, personal clothes, and jewelry into the marriage. These items, and the chest in which they were contained, would often show off her family's wealth or the young woman's skill and might even affect the success of the union. The chest was traditionally made of wood and typically decorated as richly as means would allow, the better to act as a status symbol when the bride arrived at her new home. Every suite in Al Maha is furnished with a dowry chest, and each one tells a unique tale of its distinct origin. The chests were sourced, restored, and assembled by UK artist **Lynda Shephard**. There are several types of Omani chests displayed at the hotel, brought by seafarers from India and Zanzibar. The style shown is originally from Surat, India. It is clad in brass, which was abundant in the form of studs on ships traveling between Europe and India and was believed to deflect evil, while iron was said to attract it. Brass adornment was usually a combination of thin brass plates and small upholstery-sized studs. Occasionally, a huge chest turns up with highly ornate, thick brass adornment on superbly finished hardwood, obviously for a bride from an important family. This extravagant type of piece is called a Shirazi chest.

CLOTHED IN THE CULTURE OF JORDAN

Each country in the Arab world has its own distinctive embroidery, and for thousands of years, people's origins could be identified according to the embroidery they were wearing. It is said that the patterns used in Jordan were originated by Kainan people 4,500 years ago. Al Manara's associates' uniforms provide hotel guests and global explorers an authentic journey into the country's sartorial history. **Jamal Taslaq**, Palestinian-born master couturier, was inspired to craft these designs by the breathtaking landscape surrounding Al Manara, the grandiosity of Petra and Wadi Rum, and the magical sunset over the Gulf of Aqaba. Taslaq combined the contemporary style of the West with the rich ethnic and tribal style of Jordan, selecting elements that matched the interiors and architecture of the hotel. Upon arrival, guests are welcomed by a doorman dressed in the local cavalry uniform: a black embroidered linen-blend cloak with printed artwork on its lining, as well as black wool trousers, an off-white cotton shirt, and an embroidered brown leather belt. Another custom uniform at Al Manara is that of the receptionist: a black crêpe semi-tunic with black trousers. The tunic features handmade embroidery, satin at the wrists, and a Jordanian motif on the button.

RELAXING LIKE
A LEBANESE EMIR

Grand Hills is a treasure trove of antiques from all over the world, personally curated by its owner, an avid collector. Every piece of furniture found in the hotel lobby is a piece of art in itself, which makes entering it akin to walking through a museum. One element on display—the sole piece from Lebanon, in fact—is Emir Fakhr-al-Din II's sitting room couch, a piece from his period of rule during the 1590s. Fakhr-al-Din II was an early leader of the Mount Lebanon Emirate, a self-governed area that was part of the Ottoman Empire. He was considered by some as the First Man of Lebanon, having fought the empire to unite the Lebanese people and bring sovereignty to the state. When the emir was exiled to Italy by the Ottoman regime, this couch, made by a Lebanese artisan in the 1590s, was among the personal belongings he took with him and later brought back to Lebanon years later.

LANTERNS LIGHT
THE WAY TO AJMAN

The Arabic lanterns placed in all of Ajman Saray's rooms and suites were designed by **Maurice Brill Lighting Design** and are the embodiment of the resort logo. Back in the old days, people in the Ajman region traveled with lanterns at night and used them to walk to the mosque at dawn. The lanterns symbolize hope, lighting the way in darkness, and they tie in with the hotel's philosophy of providing an enchanting coastal sanctuary, a place for people looking to escape the bustle of the city. The lanterns' light provides a soothing ambience to each room, especially at night, bringing guests relaxation and peace.

THE FORESIGHT FALCON

This unique piece, a falcon sculpture encrusted with 95,000 hand-applied Swarovski Elements crystals and designed by jeweler **Priya Chellani**, has been displayed at Grosvenor House since 2007. The work celebrates the rich cultural heritage of the regal creature it portrays, the national bird of the United Arab Emirates and an icon of force and courage in Arab culture. Before more modern hunting weapons were invented, the peregrine falcon was indispensable to Bedouin hunters for its ability to see great distances. The Foresight Falcon, displayed in the lobby of Tower 1, was part of the "Flight of Falcons" public art celebration, which included a parade of one hundred art pieces depicting falcons. Each of these was an original artwork by one of sixty artists from more than thirty countries. The falcons were all generously sponsored and have or will be auctioned to raise funds for Dubai-based charities. Proceeds from the Foresight Falcon's sale went to Foresight, an organization working to find a cure for blindness.

TRADITIONAL ETHIOPIAN TIBEB

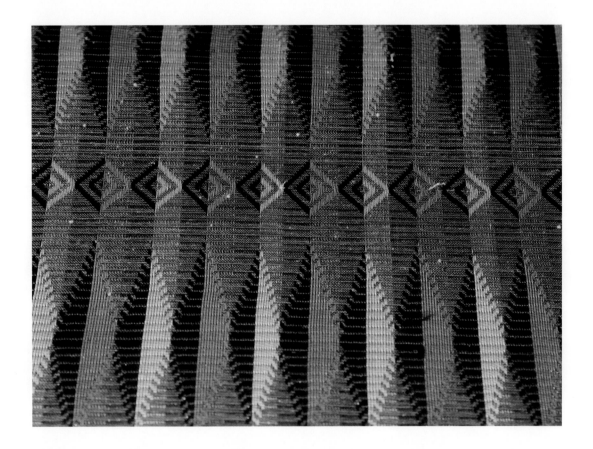

All the floors of the Sheraton Addis are adorned with *tibeb*, traditional Ethiopian designs created with fringed cloth handmade by **the expert weavers of the Dorze village**. The patterns date back to the nineteenth century, and each of the more than eighty ethnic groups in Ethiopia is represented by a different motif. All classes, from peasants to nobility, wear *tibeb*-inspired designs in different colors and patterns on their clothing to denote their social status. More complex patterns are generally reserved for higher classes. The hotel staff wears garments bearing these designs on holidays and during special events.

SETTING THE SCENE FOR A KUWAITI WEDDING

The Sheraton Kuwait's Diamond Grand Ballroom is a prime location for Kuwaiti weddings. At 2,805 square feet and with-space for two thousand guests, it needed a sophisticated light fixture that would complete its mood and provide an artistic focal point. The ballroom's splendid 24-karat-gold plated Maria Theresa chandelier, the biggest in the region at the time of its installation in 2001, was manufactured by Austrian lighting company **Dotzauer** and weighs two and a half tons. Its twenty-three-foot span incorporates 498 candles and 3,600 Swarovski crystals. This astounding piece took more than 2,800 hours to complete. The theatrical style and skill of its designer make this chandelier a true master-piece that highlights the ballroom's elegance. Its luminous glow creates an extraordinary wedding ambience.

ASIA

THE ANDAMAN

LANGKAWI, MALAYSIA

CONSERVING MALAYSIA'S CORAL

During low tide, The Andaman removes dead coral from the eight-thousand-year-old reef on its property and offers educational coral walks to guests so they can learn about this fragile ecosystem. The reef was badly damaged by the 2004 tsunami that hit Malaysia, so the resort's environmental team also conducts experiments to save pieces of live coral by transplantation and restore the reef that protects the property. In 2010, marine ecologist **Dr. Gerry Goeden** specially designed a coral nursery, believed to be the first of its kind in Southeast Asia, to rehabilitate transplanted coral for the resort's coral conservation project. The nursery consists of a makeshift ocean ecosystem designed to mimic the natural activities that occur in the ocean. To date, more than two hundred corals from the nursery have been moved back into the ocean after four to twelve months of nurturing, and the nursery currently houses about one hundred baby corals. Guests visiting the nursery are encouraged to participate in growing corals and to help nurture the new polyps. Visitors are awed by the restoration effort and excited to play their part in learning about and helping to save the reef.

THE LAGUNA
NUSA DUA, BALI, INDONESIA

DEPICTING THE GODDESS DANU

Bali is widely known for its crafts and artistry. Many internationally acclaimed artists have used its beautiful beaches and rice terraces, as well as its rich culture and traditions, as their inspiration. The lobby of The Laguna contains an enchanting mural carved from stone that depicts the epic story of the goddess Danu. Danu is one representation of the god Vishnu, who maintains the peace and harmony of each element in the universe and is one of the three gods in Balinese Hinduism, along with Brahma and Shiva. A key role of the goddess Danu is to be a guardian of justice, ensuring that nature is cultivated properly. Karma, another integral part of Balinese Hinduism, comes into play here. Mankind's selfishness will lead to natural disaster, while wisdom will lead to natural prosperity. At the center of this cycle is Danu. Guests can find out more about the stone carving by joining one of the resort tours offered on Wednesdays and Sundays.

THE ATHENEE HOTEL

BANGKOK, THAILAND

EMBROIDERY FIT FOR A PRINCESS

In The Athenee Hotel's lobby and at the top of its grand staircase, framed pieces of embroidered cloth hark back to an art practiced by aristocratic Thai women at the turn of the twentieth century. At that time, the plot of land on which the hotel now stands comprised the palace and gardens of Princess Valaya Alongkorn, daughter of King Rama V. Distinguished ladies as well as craftspeople would exercise great skill and patience to create swaths of exquisitely embroidered cloth that added a charming aesthetic to cushion covers, clothes, table coverings, and other items in common view. Reprising the muted cream-and-ivory color schemes and royal and religious motifs of Princess Valaya's era, the embroideries in the hotel's collection are made of silk interwoven with golden threading, embossed with pearls, and pleated to create a vivid relief effect. The pieces were handmade by students majoring in textile, costume, and garment and fashion design in the **Faculty of Fine and Applied Arts at Thammasat University**, and each one took about two weeks to complete. The designs required meticulous research of illustrated accounts of Princess Valaya's palace and scanning actual remnants. Great care was taken to be as true to the originals as possible, from the selection of raw materials to the creation of the fabric using period-appropriate tools.

A WALL OF SILK

Hangzhou, known as the "home of silk," has played an important role in China's traditional weaving industry for 4,700 years. The secret to silk production is the silkworm—the caterpillar phase of the silk moth *Bombyx mori*—which feeds solely on the leaves of mulberry trees. The Chinese use silk for art and decorations, as well as for clothing. In the past, silk was an integral part of the Chinese economy; caravans traded the prized fabrics along the famed Silk Road into the Near East. By the fourth century BC, Alexander the Great is said to have introduced silk to Europe, where its popularity was influenced by Christian prelates, who donned the rich fabrics and adorned their altars with them. The nobility also began to have their clothing fashioned from silk fabrics. The Azure Qiantang's lobby design, with its silk wall created by **Wang Xue from Mai Lu Art Design Studio**, is inspired by a poem called "Beauty of the South," by Bai Juyi, a famous poet of the Tang dynasty: "At sunrise, the river flows redder than flames; in spring, the river water is the blue of azure." It incorporates the acanthus, the city flower that is sweet-smelling and brings good luck, and the hotel's signature blue shade to present a true Hangzhou welcome to hotel guests. Like so many strands of silk, the lobby weaves together important pillars of Chinese culture: art, weaving, trade, and poetry.

LIGHTING INSPIRED BY LANDSCAPE

Because Hongta Group is a subordinate enterprise of China Tobacco Yunnan Industrial Company, it was established in the city of Yuxi, the hometown of Yunnan tobacco. Yunnan is a province of China with a varied landscape that includes mountains, rice terraces, lakes, rivers, and gorges. Thus, designer **Matthew Lui of Hirsch Bedner Associates** used natural and botanical elements in the lobby. The large chandelier was created in the form of a leaf. A diffusion of bronze and marble textures and a cloudlike pattern give a classic and elegant feel that ties in with the landscape. While nature itself has been creating treasures in this image for thousands of years, it is extraordinarily rare for a leaf to be rendered so beautifully in marble.

THE ITALIAN RENAISSANCE IN CHINA

Dalian, unique among Chinese cities for its eclectic blend of European, Russian, and Japanese architecture, has been an international trading hub for centuries. Nestled in the lobby of The Castle Hotel is an Italian ormolu-mounted ivory and hardstone–inlaid ebony and ebonized cabinet, which matches the color scheme of the Negro Marquina and gold Calacatta marble floor. This antique piece, one of sixty-nine displayed at the hotel, was acquired by the Reverend Honourable Edward Vesey Bligh, son of Edward, 5th Earl of Darnley, and was later purchased by an auction agency hired to collect antiques for The Castle Hotel to curate as its own personal museum, reflecting the diverse city surrounding it. During the second half of the nineteenth century, craftsmen often reinterpreted or combined the forms and motifs of both classical and Renaissance art. The cabinet was built during this time and is most likely from Florence. It features an abundance of semiprecious stones among ivory-inlaid foliage and is inspired by the certosina-style inlaid furniture of the Italian High Renaissance.

CAPTURING THE FLOWER OF NANJING

Two paintings of plum blossoms, the flower of the city of Nanjing, decorate the Grand Mansion's south entrance. The works were made especially for the hotel by **Cao Yue**, an artist and teacher at the Shanghai Academy of Fine Arts whose work combines both traditional Chinese art and composite materials. The paintings were created directly on wood instead of canvas. The artist used different types of paint, including *qi*, traditional Chinese paint extracted from the qi tree that is totally natural, with no chemicals. He also used duck egg for the plum blossoms to achieve their exact texture and aesthetic. The plum blossom remains a captivating subject. Plum Blossom Hill, one of Nanjing's famous sightseeing spots, is about a twenty-minute drive from the hotel. Every year in February and March, when the blossoms come, this site receives more than 100,000 visitors per day.

RUTH POWYS
chief executive of Elephant Family

DO YOU HAVE A FAVORITE ITEM OR COLLECTIBLE THAT YOU ALWAYS SEEK OUT WHEN TRAVELING?

If I'm traveling into wilderness, I have a constant suppressed desire to take something from the earth: stones, fossils, shells.... But as this is not very conservation friendly, my favorite collectibles turn out to be humans, often amazing guides who have no point of comparison with their world and the rest of the planet. I love inviting them to London, introducing their world to mine, and forming lifelong friendships with the people who protect these special places.

WHY DO YOU LIKE TO COLLECT THESE ITEMS FROM YOUR TRAVELS?

It can be empty to travel without real, deep connection, to leave a place having been shown around and having made a thin connection with the people there. We are so lucky, and life is so much more fun when you share.

DO YOU HAVE ANY FAVORITE LOCAL MEMENTOS THAT YOU HAVE COLLECTED FROM YOUR TRAVELS? WHY ARE THEY SPECIAL? WHERE ARE THEY FROM?

My favorite person memento was when two Maasai warriors came to London and absolutely fell in love with the National Portrait Gallery. A bright green, fully inflated rubber ring that hangs on our living room wall is my favorite of all my travel treasures. My husband is from South India, where swimming lessons were uncommon when he was a little boy. Our first holiday together was in Greece. He was so self-conscious about not being able to swim. The rubber ring was the answer. It was the first time he felt the sensation of floating in water: to him, utter magic.

HOW DO YOU LIKE TO CURATE, ORGANIZE, OR DISPLAY KEEPSAKES FROM YOUR TRAVELS AT HOME?

I hang treasures up the stairs, the best from each trip—photographs, spears, tribal masks, maps.... It's a restless and endless edit involving lots of paint and potholes!

TIPU'S TIGER TOYS

In the heritage city of Srirangapatna, legend has it that a formidable ruler during the eighteenth century, Tipu Sultan, was known as the Tiger of Mysore after he brought down one of these majestic beasts with nothing more than a dagger. Thus, the tiger is a motif across the the state of Karnataka, in southwest India. Part of the philosophy of ITC Hotels is that the high-quality experiences they offer do not in any way burden the environment or surrounding society. Initiatives such as WelcomArt mirror this goal and focus on promoting art and culture in India. Crafted by local artisans based in Channapatna, the tiger figurine and tiger lounge chairs in ITC Gardenia's grand arrival court encompass both the spirit of Tipu Sultan's Karnataka and the hotel's dedication to responsible luxury.

The tiger loungers and figurine are inspired by the famous toys of Channapatna. During his reign, Tipu Sultan invited artisans from Persia to train local Indian craftsmen in the making of colorful, hand-painted wooden toys and artifacts carved from rosewood. One special piece created for the ruler, now exhibited at the Victoria and Albert Museum in London, is called *Tipu's Tiger* and depicts a tiger savaging a near-life-size European man. Mechanisms inside the man's body make his hand move and his mouth emit a wailing sound, and a mechanism inside the tiger produces grunting noises. This piece expresses Tipu Sultan's hatred for British rule during colonial times. Channapatna toys are available at the local shops in Karnataka, though the model on display at ITC Gardenia is not allowed to be imitated.

ITC GRAND BHARAT

GURGAON, HARYANA, INDIA

A SPIRITUAL STAIRCASE

Ghats are flights of stone steps along the bank of the Ganges where pilgrims perform ritual ablutions. For Hindus, the ghats are locations on the divine cosmic road, indicative of its manifest transcendental dimension. The city of Varanasi has at least eighty-four ghats. According to Hindu beliefs, a celestial beauty known as the Yamuna came down from the heavens to purify the earth. In sacred texts, she is the holder of infinite love and compassion from having lapped the shores of Lord Krishna's village, Vrindavan. Lord Krishna played along the Keshi Ghat, Vrindavan's principal bathing place, which leads down to the Yamuna river, the longest and second-largest tributary of the Ganges. The Yamuna runs on ITC Grand Bharat's property, separating the public from the private sphere, and **Jim Nordlie at Archiventure Group** created the hotel's own private Yamuna Ghat, made of native sandstone, in the image of those in Varanasi. Every evening, as dusk descends, the *aarti*, a religious ritual of worship, is performed at the Yamuna Ghat by a local priest. This powerful, uplifting, and soulful experience begins when a tall lamp is lit and a salver is prepared with marigolds. The priest blows a conch shell and waves the lamp toward the holy water of the river. Votive candles are prepared to sit in nests of dry leaves and marigold flowers, and guests are invited to float the candles in the river. Finally, sweetmeats are served as guests and staff enjoy the visual delight of the candles floating in the rippling water.

EMBROIDERED ELEMENTS: PARSI GARA SAREES

ITC Grand Central is designed to bring guests back to Old Bombay, a time during which the Parsi community was a prominent part of the city's development. They brought sarees embellished with *gara* embroidery (the term stems from a Gujarati word for saree)—traditionally worn by women during festive occasions—from China into India in the mid-nineteenth century. Classic gara sarees were handwoven with natural Chinese silk in shades of magenta, royal blue, turquoise, and red and were embellished with handmade embroidery. This made them very heavy and uncomfortable to walk in, as well as extremely expensive. The modern-day gara is made with either crepe or georgette so as to be lighter, but the traditional embroidery motifs have not changed and include birds, fauna, and flowers—often roses, jasmine, and chrysanthemums are woven in groups of thirty to represent angels, one for each day of the month, as a good omen. The hotel's guest relations executives wear gara sarees sold by local shop **Mahavir Emporium**—whose proprietor also owns the workshop that produces them—to reflect the rich culture of the Parsis.

MAHAVIR EMPORIUM

Shop No. 226/30,
Kalbadrvi Road
Mumbai, Maharashtra 400002
India
+91 22 2240 5061

ITC GRAND CHOLA

CHENNAI, TAMIL NADU, INDIA

A CHOLA CHARIOT OF VICTORY

On the grand staircase of ITC Grand Chola's Sangam Lobby sits the Chariot of Victory, a display featuring two sets of ornate metallic wheels and horses. These pieces are reproductions of sculptures found inside two of the most iconic Chola temples in Tamil Nadu: The wheels come from Airavatesvara Temple in Darasuram, which was built by Rajaraja Chola II in the twelfth century, and the horses are from Nageswaraswamy Temple in Kumbakonam, built by Aditya Chola I in the ninth century. The Chariot of Victory embodies the influence and expanse of the Chola dynasty, which lasted for more than 1,500 years. Master sculptor **Sthapathi Ravindran** created the relief in the ancient style of lost-wax casting and cast it in Panchaloha, an amalgamation of copper, zinc, lead, silver, and gold that is sacred and symbolic in Hindu tradition. Ravindran's lineage dates back to the Chola empire, which ended in 1279.

ITC KAKATIYA

HYDERABAD, TELANGANA, INDIA

A ROYAL COURT
IN THE KAKATIYA DYNASTY

Queen Rani Rudrama Devi ruled in the thirteenth century during the Kakatiya dynasty, which laid the foundation for a golden era in Telangana's history. ITC Kakatiya has paid tribute to this time by decorating its lobby as a replica of the queen's court, including the Kakatiya Kala Thoranam, also called the Kakatiya Victory Gate or Warangal Gate, a historical arch in the state's Warangal district. The gate, conceptualized by the hotel's interior decorator, Francesca Basu, was built from plaster of paris and symbolizes the dynasty's golden era.

ITC MARATHA

MUMBAI, MAHARASHTRA, INDIA

SILK STYLES: PAITHANI SAREES

Every corner of ITC Maratha preserves the traditions of Maharashtra. *Paithani* sarees date back more than two thousand years, and their rich weave and colorful silk make them the most precious heirloom a Maratha woman owns. These sarees, displayed in the hotel lobby and worn by the hotel's guest relations executives, are handmade by artisan **Vijaya Bhagwat** of Yeola, a nearby town known for its pure silk and traditional weaving methods. The garments require careful hand movements and foot-eye coordination, and depending on how thorough the detailing is, the creation process could take anywhere from a month to two years. First, the raw silk threads are dyed with tints from vegetables, minerals, and plants, and the colors are then used in combination. Two color threads are used lengthwise and a third color is used widthwise while weaving. The preparation of the loom, which takes an entire day, is probably the most painstaking part of the process, as it determines the design, color, and finer details of the finished product.

The most distinguishing feature of a paithani saree is the *pallu*, or loose end. The borders of the pallu are created with an interlocked weft technique, either with colored silk or *zari*, fine gold or silver thread. In a border woven with zari, colored silk patterns are added, usually in the form of a flower or a creeping vine. Popular pallu motifs include Mor (peacock), Bangadi Mor (bangle with four peacocks and lotus), Munia/Tota-Maina (parrot), Ajanta (lotus), Asavali (vines and flowers), Koyari (mango shape), and Akruti (almond shape). ITC Maratha extends a warm welcome by giving guests their own paithani saree, connecting them with Maratha culture.

ITC MAURYA

NEW DELHI, INDIA

A MURAL OF
THE MAURYAN DYNASTY

ITC is the first hospitality group to underscore the significance of contemporary Indian art, and the architecture and interiors of ITC Maurya were inspired by the ancient Mauryan dynasty. While the hotel's exterior is based on Buddhist stupas from the third century BC, the central lobby re-creates the paneled dome of a chaitya, or Buddhist hall of worship, complete with a splendid painted mural titled *The Great Procession*. Created by celebrated Indian artist **Krishen Khanna**, the three-thousand-square-foot work took about five years to complete and depicts, in the artist's words, "The great procession that is India and Indian life." For more than sixty decades, Khanna has painted the faces and figures of India, striving to freeze on canvas the country's richness of humanity in all of its varied color and form. The theme of this mural has universal appeal: a moving, animated procession of contemporary figures, some known—such as Mauryan Emperor Ashoka and his edicts, who spread the Buddhist message of peace throughout the kingdom—and others anonymous, set into an urban setting that flows into landscapes of water and sky. The drama that unfolds within the artwork is a true experience that each visitor can interpret in his or her own way.

ITC MUGHAL

AGRA, UTTAR PRADESH, INDIA

THE POMEGRANATE: A MAGICAL FRUIT

ITC Mughal is a magnificent oasis of tranquility modeled on gardens laid out by the Mughal dynasty. Babur, the first Mughal emperor, brought paradise gardens to India. With channels of running water, fountains, fragrant flowers, and fruit trees, these spaces were meant to be lived in. It is also believed that Babur brought the pomegranate from his homeland, Ferghana. In tribute to him, this delicious fruit is the theme of Kaya Kalp: The Royal Spa, a 99,000-square-foot space worthy of its regal title. Built by architect **Pradeep Sachdeva**, the spa, which is itself surrounded by pomegranate trees, features a reception area with a bold frieze of ruby red pomegranates along the wall and ceiling. This motif is repeated in the white terrazzo flooring inlaid with red stone.

The pomegranate and its nutritious qualities are also highlighted in the spa's treatments, which are offered by specially trained therapist **Waraporn Thatsanadee**. The luxurious pomegranate Aromasoul massage serves to detoxify, revitalize, and elevate the senses. Kaya Kalp's signature blend of pomegranate, lime, ginger, and organic brown sugar deeply cleanses, polishes, and softens the body to perfection, leaving the skin glowing and vibrant. The Pomegranate Bath Infusion, used in bathing water, is a natural essence high in antioxidants, amino acids, and vitamins B and C that renews the skin, allows it to heal faster, and helps fight signs of aging. Pure pomegranate juice is also served as a welcoming beverage as guests enter the spa.

DRESSING THE PART: BALUCHARI SAREES

ITC Sonar looks back to the days when the *bhadralok*, or Bengali gentlefolk, reigned supreme. To preserve the region's intrinsic flavor and textile heritage, the hotel's guest relations executives wear silk *baluchari* sarees, traditional garments donned by Bengali nobles for celebrations and festivals. These sarees were originally woven under the patronage of the Nawabs of Murshidabad, a town in West Bengal, and take their name from the town of Baluchar, near Murshidabad. The garments have floral borders and elaborate *aanchal*, or ends, with animal motifs, taking inspiration from the terra-cotta temples of Bishnupur, a small town in the Bankura district of West Bengal. Paisley is also a popular motif. During the Nawabi era, the patterns included human figures with nawabs, or governors, and their begums, or ladies of high rank. Later, *baluchari* sarees made during the patronage of the East India Company featured European motifs and figures. The hotel's saree design was woven by artisans at the **Crafts Council of West Bengal**, a nongovernmental organization that sustains and promotes Bengali arts and crafts. The design selected is more than one hundred years old and is not available anywhere else.

ITC WINDSOR

BENGALURU, KARNATAKA, INDIA

A SCENE FROM
THE EDWARDIAN ERA

ITC Windsor's restaurant, Dum Pukht Jolly Nabobs, was designed by Francesca Basu and re-creates in exquisite detail a formal regimental dining scene from the early years of the Edwardian era. One of the dining room's focal points is a chromolithographic print capturing the coronation of His Majesty King Edward VII and Queen Alexandra at Westminster Abbey in London on August 9, 1902. Estimated to be 115 years old, this rare print was sourced from a specialized antiques dealer in the United Kingdom to add to the room's authentic charm. Chromolithography refers to all types of lithography printed in color. Lithographers sought a way to work on flat surfaces with the use of chemicals instead of using raised relief or recessed intaglio techniques, and thus chromolithography was born. Along with the print, the chandeliers, the tables in the style of the Tudor era, the exposed rafters, the porcelain flatware, and the paneled wainscoting all combine to transport diners back in time.

A RAJASTHANI ROYAL PROCESSION

Upon entering ITC Rajputana's lobby, guests will immediately notice two murals by local artist **Shri Kripal Singh Shekhawat**. Wall hangings and murals are traditional in Rajasthan, and most of the state's royal families have commissioned artists to paint such works for their *haveli* (mansion) homes. The ones at the hotel depict Maharaja Jai Singh, who ruled in the eighteenth century and founded Jaipur, celebrating his victory in battle against Bundi State. The writing above each work is in Dingal, an ancient Indian language written in Nagri script. The artist worked painstakingly on the lobby wall with wet pigments for about six months to create these pieces, using Rajasthan's traditional Phad painting style and vibrant, earthy colors.

KERATON AT THE PLAZA

JAKARTA, INDONESIA

A STUDY IN JAVANESE STYLE

The lobby of Keraton at the Plaza, adorned with magnificent artwork, has become its guests' favorite location for meetings. At the entrance hangs **Grahacipta Hadiprana**'s bold, eight-foot-tall *bunga kawung*–motif crystal chandelier, its traditional style celebrating simple elegance and classical shapes. The lobby's backdrop is the floor-to-ceiling *batik kawung* artwork, beautifully accentuated on each side by two *pusaka kacumas* sculptures, which symbolize purity. All of the art, created by local artists, is curated by Hadiprana's Jakarta-based design firm and reflects power, wealth, and elegance, observing the rich traditions of central Java.

A XIANG EMBROIDERY WELCOME

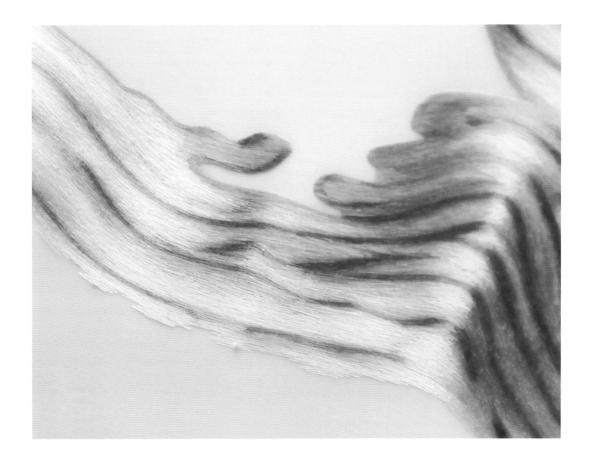

With more than 2,500 years of history, Xiang embroidery is known as one of the four most distinguished embroidery styles in China. Its character is lifelike, with bright, vivid patterns. A Xiang embroidery pendant made in a design known as the Double Fish is placed at the entrance to each guest room to bring good luck and happiness. This design harks back to one of the hotel's inspirations: the Peaches of Immortality, known in Chinese mythology as special fruits that the Jade Emperor and Empress gave to the deities to make them immortal. In the same way, the embroidered pendant sends good wishes from the hotel to its guests, offering gracious hospitality. Guests feel welcomed by this kind sentiment and often want to find their own works of embroidery during their stay in Changsha.

A GONG FOR DRAGON SPIRITS

Ancient legends tell that long, long ago there was a mythical dragon roaming around the Andaman Sea, and upon seeing the particularly beautiful area where The Naka Island is found today, with its wonderful views of Phang Nga Bay and its ever-changing sunrises and sunsets, he decided that this was where he would lie for his remaining days. When the enormous mythical dragon passed away, he turned into an island of stone, rock, and sand. Over many years, due to erosion and weather, this land separated into three smaller islands, which can still be seen today as Koh Rad (the dragon's head), Koh Naka Yai (the resort's island, the dragon's body), and Koh Naka Noi (the dragon's tail).

For centuries, gongs have been viewed as a symbol of status and wealth among Thai families, and ringing one is thought to bring good luck, health, and happiness. In ancient times, it was believed that a gong could be used for communicating with mystical spirits from different realms. The story of The Naka Island includes a belief that the dragon's spirit is still here. Upon the arrival of guests to the island, the staff bangs the resort's special hammered-brass gong once to honor the dragon so he will look after the guests during their adventures, and then a second time to allow the visitors to make a wish and have the dragon help it come true. Upon their departure from the island, the gong is hit once more to ensure a safe return voyage and bid a warm farewell and thank-you to the dragon.

THE SECRET TO TARU SAKE

Sake, a fermented alcohol made from rice, has many varieties, including Junmai-shu, Honjozo-shu, and Ginjo-shu. Each has a different brewing process and level of rice polish. Taru sake, Prince Gallery Tokyo's signature beverage, is characterized by its aroma of wood, which comes from the ripening process in a barrel made of fine Yoshino cedarwood, a species of tree local to the area. This type of sake was served at the hotel's opening, as well as at many other special events on property such as weddings and parties. It is said that the word sake comes from sakae, or prosperity, and sharing the beverage is an essential part of a joyous scene in Japan.

WEAVING A LACQUERED BASKET

Sheraton Grande Sukhumvit's restaurant, basil, features cuisines from four regions of Thailand, and all design elements were carefully selected to showcase the venue's authenticity. One decorative motif, procured from **artisans at Chatuchak Market** in Bangkok, is a lacquered basket known as a *hai*. The baskets are traditionally used in Southeast Asian homes to store rice, and they come in an array of colors, shapes, and sizes. They are traditionally made using lightweight but durable materials, such as bamboo, and coated with resin tapped from the Chinese lacquer tree, *Rhus verniciflua*. This results in a thick, dark, lustrous surface that prevents moisture, insects, and oxidation from taking hold. The hai are then decorated according to regional styles, from the rustic to the more refined.

CHATUCHAK MARKET

587/10 Kamphaeng Phet 2 Road
Khwaeng Chatuchak,
Khet Chatuchak
Krung Thep Maha Nakhon 10900
Thailand
+66 2 272 4813

Open Wednesday & Thursday
7 a.m.–6 p.m.
Friday 6 p.m.–12 a.m.
Saturday & Sunday
9 a.m.–6 p.m.

INTERPRETING TRADITIONAL JAPANESE DRAWINGS

Featured in Suiran's Gyokuto Garden Terrace Suite, on a sliding door between the bedroom and the living room, is a work of art called *Togetsu Kaboku Zu (Crossing Moon, Flower, and Trees)*, created by **Ryo Shinagawa** using traditional Japanese drawing and painting techniques. Suiran partnered with a local university to select an art student whose style fit with the hotel's design concept: inheriting and improving on the past while opening the way to the future. The piece represents scenery and the seasons of the Arashiyama district, where the hotel is located, and is especially inspired by the Hozu River. The gold leaf evokes moonlight, as the moon is an important icon in the region. The artist expresses the phases of the moon through the reflection of light, which occurs as the viewer changes position. White paint depicts flowers representing four seasons: the plum tree's blossoms for spring, morning glory for summer, chrysanthemum for fall, and camellia for winter. These distinct blooms can be identified by the shapes of their leaves. The flowers feature dots and *seigaiha*, a traditional Japanese wave design, which shows the reflection of the moonlight on the water's surface as reflected back on the flower.

THE ORIENTAL PEARL
OF SU EMBROIDERY

Su is one of China's four famous styles of embroidery and dates back more than two thousand years. It is praised as "the pearl of oriental art." The unique style of this craft fits with Twelve at Hengshan's modern-chinoiserie aesthetic and conveys the concept of East meeting West and past meeting present. The hotel's guest rooms and lobby are decorated in a soft, natural color palette offset by bespoke Chinese and contemporary furnishings. The Su embroidery pieces, with their natural patterns and vivid birds, add remarkable focal points and a distinctive Asian flourish to the atmosphere. The embroidery offers comfort to guests who feel at home surrounded by authentic Chinese artistry.

THE CREATURES
OF HIMAVANTA FOREST

Every design aspect of Vana Belle was created in close consultation with a feng shui master. The concept is based on the fabled Himmapan or Himavanta Forest, found in Hindu and Buddhist mythology, which is said to contain myriad creatures with mystical powers. Two handcrafted statues by an anonymous Thai artist who specializes in the creation of cultural and mythical symbols in metallic form, are important elements of this design. The Kunchorn Waree, or water elephant statue, found in the lobby acts as the hotel's mascot and symbolizes success. One of the beings from the mythical forest, it has the head and front legs of an elephant and the body and tail of a fish. Some speculate this may have been the only creature capable of swimming across Sithandon, an immense ocean surrounding Mount Sumeru, the center of the universe and gateway to Nirvana. It is a dramatic centerpiece for the lobby's stunning water features and a panoramic view of Chaweng Noi bay below. The Hong Jeen, or Chinese swan statue, which stands in the lobby garden, symbolizes luck, longevity, virtue, beauty, honesty, and politeness. With an air of elegance reminiscent of a regal peacock, this piece is silhouetted by the sunrise. In mythology, the Hong Jeen creates a beautiful chirping sound reminiscent of heavenly music and only visits Earth every thousand years. It is considered very fortunate to encounter this auspicious bird during a stay at Vana Belle.

EUROPE

AN AUGUSTINIAN FRESCO

Augustine was created from seven historically significant buildings, the largest and most important of which is the thirteenth-century St. Thomas Monastery, after which the hotel is named. Refectory Bar is located within the monastery in what was once a double-height vaulted refectory where monks would gather for lunch and dinner and prepare for Mass. The former refectory features beautiful nineteenth-century baroque frescoes. The ceiling depicts Augustinian symbology: a burning heart crossed by an arrow, with four angels, Raphael, Gabriel, Jophiel, and Michael, shown around the heart. Each holds an Augustinian attribute: the *mifra* (hat), *baculum* (stick), *libre* (book), and *galericulum* (belt). Augustine's bartenders have created special cocktails named for the attributes held by the angels in the fresco. Guests of Refectory Bar can also taste St. Thomas beer, which was first produced by monks in 1352 and is now only available at Augustine.

TEAS TO ENJOY IN CRETE

Blue Palace's signature tea collection, created in collaboration with renowned Greek brand **Tea Route**, is available in four different blends, all inspired by the island of Crete: Calming, Wild, Summer, and Spring. The Calming blend includes marjoram, ironwort, chamomile, and marigold; the Wild blend brings together Cretan fennel, nettle, thyme, mountain tea, sage, and chamomile; the Summer blend features green tea, mango, and apricot; and the Spring blend combines mountain tea, dittany, and orange blossom. The teas are available at the Arsenali Lounge Bar and are the perfect accompaniment to the cakes, scones, and finger sandwiches also on offer.

ARTFUL ANATOLIAN CERAMICS

Located on land renowned for its cultural heritage, Caresse has an architectural style evocative of the low-rise hillside villages that punctuate the Turkish coastline. With the azure of the Aegean Sea as its backdrop, the resort's color palette is derived directly from its surroundings, featuring hues of ochre and stone that pair with the area's verdant tropical plants and vibrant bougainvillea. As a complement to its traditional Turkish architecture, Caresse displays handmade Anatolian ceramics created by artist **Tülay Özgür**. The style, design, and decoration of these ceramics is quite distinctive from the era of Seljuk civilization techniques, building on and modernizing designs from the eleventh century. Inspired by the Aegean Sea and the blue skies of Bodrum, these eye-catching jewels of contemporary art fit effortlessly with Caresse's design and are on view in the resort's art gallery.

A ROYAL HUNT
IN SALÓN ANCKERMANN

Castillo Hotel Son Vida's Salón Anckermann, used for elegant celebrations such as weddings and anniversaries, is adorned with **Ricard Anckermann**'s original paintings from 1903. Anckermann is considered one of the most important Mallorcan artists of all time. At the turn of the century, Ferran Truyols Despuig, the Marqués de la Torre, owner of Son Vida and avid hunter, commissioned Anckermann to decorate the hotel's dining room. This was the artist's last major project, finished three years before his death. The work consists of canvases mounted on frames that depict ten scenes from a royal hunting expedition in the eighteenth century: *The Departure from the Castle, Riding to the Hunting Grounds, The Pursuit of Game, A Bolting Horse, The Prince and His Bride, Open-Air Cooking, Banquet, Dancing, Games,* and *The Return to the Castle.* In contrast to his previous works, the painter here entirely dispenses with heavy symbolism and concentrates his efforts on a naturalistic portrayal. At the beginning of the twentieth century, the region was focused on agriculture—hunting is still a popular pastime on Mallorca today—so it was common to decorate a dining or living room in this way.

CRISTALLO

CORTINA D'AMPEZZO, ITALY

A FANTASY RIDE
IN THE DOLOMITES

Cristallo's lobby displays a hand-carved wooden ski luge by **Mauro Lampo**. Made exclusively for the resort and complete with the Cristallo logo, this piece recalls the surrounding mountain range, the Dolomites. Made from a local variety of Swiss stone pine wood, called *cirmolo* in Italian, the ski luge fits with the resort's design theme, carrying local nature indoors. Lampo's process is very hands-on and collaborative, and he even lets visitors to his workshop participate in carving some of the pieces he works on.

THE ART OF GLASS

Excelsior Hotel Gallia's interior celebrates the timeless elegance of the Art Deco period. The staggering eighty-two-foot Murano glass chandelier placed over the grand staircase captures the hotel's soul and glittering style. This bespoke piece, crafted by high-end lighting manufacturer **De Majo**, consists of more than 2,600 pounds of light and glass fragments that alternate harmoniously, giving guests an exceptional welcome indeed. The chandelier's cascade of lights connects all floors of the hotel, bringing the staircase to life and offering a dazzling photo opportunity. And the illuminating magic of De Majo also extends to the hotel's restaurant, suites, and spa, for which the company produced ten different types of lighting fixtures, each creating just the right mood and ambience.

DE MAJO SHOWROOM
Via Galileo Galilei, 34
30035 Murano, Venice
Italy
+39 041 57 29 617
demajoilluminazione.com

Open Monday–Friday
9 a.m.–1 p.m.
and 2–6 p.m.

REPURPOSING CAVE ROCK

When Falisia was constructed, a great deal of cave rock was removed from the property. Slovenian artist **Damjan Komel** repurposed some of the stones to make his work *Prince on the Bollard*, a frog prince sitting on a bollard, or a post found on a wharf or ship's deck to which a rope may be secured. This piece is one of a series by Komel depicting animals sitting on bollards, many of which can be found around the area of Portopiccolo, a little village on the Gulf of Trieste. Falisia is right on the marina, and its furniture and overall shape are reminiscent of a cruise ship, so *Prince on the Bollard* is the perfect fit. Komel's artistic vision was based on his passion for Alexander Pushkin's novels and the idea that everyone should find a way to be safely anchored in the harbor of life, a view the hotel shares with its guests.

MARIA THERESA'S ROSE

Bratislava flourished under the Austro-Hungarian monarchy, especially during the eighteenth-century reign of Maria Theresa. Under her watch, green public areas emerged, and the first gardens in the style of Versailles, filled with orange trees and rose bushes, came to Bratislava Castle. Back then, the Danube flowed where the Grand Hotel River Park stands today. In the nineteenth century, Count Enea Grazioso Lanfranconi, builder and waterworks expert, proposed that the river's course be adjusted so that it no longer washed the castle hill. Dog roses grew on the embankment, which was created to regulate the river's flow and is the site of the hotel. The rose was Maria Theresa's favorite flower, and it became the hotel's symbol. **Gordana Turuk at Gordana Glass** created a glass rose especially for the Grand Hotel River Park to display in the lobby as a reminder of the city's rich history and the importance of passing it on to future generations. Turuk's piece is made with laid glass painted with gold and rose gold.

THE GRITTI PALACE
VENICE, ITALY

VENICE'S FINEST FABRICS

To demonstrate the close link between The Gritti Palace and the artisans of Venice, The Gritti has always been dressed by Venice's famous artisan textile houses. For The Gritti's restoration in 2013, **the Rubelli Group** supplied almost seven and a half miles of material. The textiles outfit the hotel's spaces in different moods, creating a balance with all other design features. These silk, velvet, and embroidered damask fabrics appear in two hundred patterns throughout the hotel: in furniture, curtains, wall hangings, and bedspreads. They create a welcoming, residential feel more akin to a luxurious private palace than a hotel. All Rubelli fabrics are reproductions of exclusive designs documented in the Venetian *maison*'s archives and woven at the Rubelli mill in Cucciago, in the province of Como. The Gritti's flame-retardant fabrics in Trevira CS were woven from fine yarns on looms normally used for weaving silk, producing materials with a silky effect and a pleasant feel. The Baccarat design, a revival of a rich, precious lampas dating back to the eighteenth century, can be found in the hotel's Club del Doge restaurant, while Nastri is a fabric created exclusively for some of The Gritti's guest rooms.

RUBELLI SHOWROOM

Piscina S. Samuele
San Marco
3393 Venice
Italy
rubelli.com

MARGHERITA MACCAPANI MISSONI
fashion designer, model, and actress

DO YOU HAVE A FAVORITE ITEM OR COLLECTIBLE THAT YOU ALWAYS SEEK OUT WHEN TRAVELING?

I collect several things, but I particularly enjoy collecting fake flowers, which I often seem to find during my trips.

WHY DO YOU LIKE TO COLLECT THESE ITEMS FROM YOUR TRAVELS?

I like the fact that when I display all of these fake flowers in my home, they look like a cohesive, fully realized collection, but each one tells a different, unique story, reminding me of my many memorable travels.

DO YOU HAVE ANY FAVORITE LOCAL MEMENTOS THAT YOU HAVE COLLECTED FROM YOUR TRAVELS? WHY ARE THEY SPECIAL? WHERE ARE THEY FROM?

Recently in Bolivia, I bought some incredible masks that are traditionally used in Oruro during Carnaval. They are so vibrant and fun—I couldn't hold back.

HOW DO YOU LIKE TO CURATE, ORGANIZE, OR DISPLAY KEEPSAKES FROM YOUR TRAVELS AT HOME?

I just moved into a new home, and I have decided to fill one of the bathrooms with all the kitsch souvenirs I have acquired from my travels around the world: religious artifacts, ex-votos, and porte-bonheur charms. This way, I can enjoy them daily, while they don't annoy my husband.

IS THERE SOMETHING THAT YOU HAVE COVETED FROM A HOTEL OR A HOTEL ROOM?

The Murano chandelier at The Gritti Palace in Venice.

WHAT ARE YOUR TIPS FOR TRAVELERS WHO WANT TO BRING HOME A UNIQUE AND AUTHENTIC SOUVENIR?

Head to the local market!

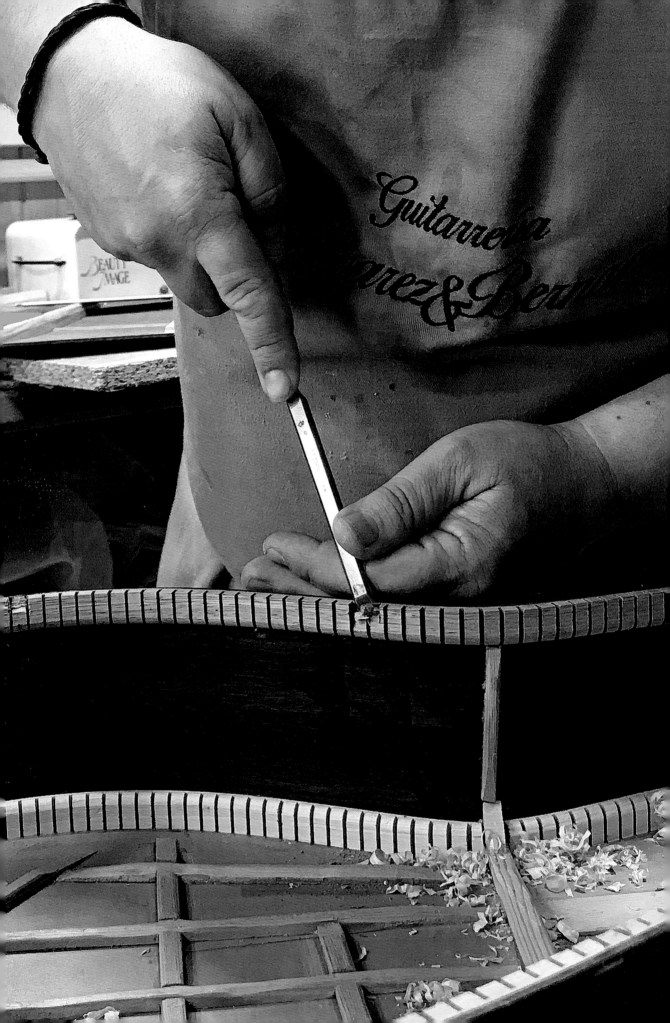

CREATING THE SPANISH SOUND

Seville boasts a rich, deeply rooted musical tradition that highlights flamenco, which is characterized by the Spanish guitar. **Antonio Bernal of Guitarrería Álvarez & Bernal** created one of these prized instruments especially for Hotel Alfonso XIII's lobby. The main differences between the two types of Spanish guitars—flamenco and classical—are found in the types of wood and the construction of harmonic bars (pieces of wood placed inside the top plate of the guitar that support the tension of the strings and affect timbre). The wood for each instrument—Palo Santo from Brazil or German spruce, for example—is carefully selected and can be cured for up to twenty years. The choice of wood is significant because it dictates thickness, angles, and numerous other features that affect the guitar's sound. The flamenco guitar typically produces a sharp and smooth bass and is easier to play. Upon visiting Bernal's atelier, guests can see the great effort and time that go into just one of these distinctive pieces. Visitors are dazzled by the precision and care required to make an instrument that both fully encapsulates Seville's heritage and creates beautiful music. On special nights, Hotel Alfonso XIII has a musician play the Spanish guitar on the patio.

GUITARRERÍA ÁLVAREZ & BERNAL

Calle Hernando del Pulgar, 20, 41007 Seville, Spain
+34 954 58 26 79
guitarreriaalvarezybernal.com

Open Monday–Friday 10 a.m.–2 p.m.and 5–8 p.m.
Saturday 10 a.m.–1:30 p.m.

AUSTRIA'S ELITE AT THE TURN OF THE CENTURY

In 1910, Austrian landscape and portrait painter **Hans Stalzer** was a good friend of The Bristol's owner, Arthur Wolf, as well as a regular guest at the hotel. Stalzer was inspired by all of the famous personalities who also stayed there—Theodore Roosevelt, Baroness Thyssen-Bornemisza, Oskar Kokoschka, Adolf Loos, Baroness Bertha von Suttner, and Archduke Franz Salvator, to name just a few—and he painted a number of them in the grand dining room during one of the archduke's dinners. Like no other painting of its time, Stalzer's work provides insight into the nightly society gatherings at The Bristol in the early twentieth century, as well as the fashions of the time. The maître d'hôtel and his waiters are among the thirty-six people included in the painting, a practice that was quite unusual back then. This reflects the strong collaboration between the staff and owner and shows Mr. Wolf's appreciation of his team. The painting is a welcome addition to the hotel's mezzanine, as it still reflects The Bristol's atmosphere today: high-quality, discreet service; personal attention; and welcoming Austrian hospitality.

MAGNIFYING THE COSMOS

Since its opening in 1901, Hotel Bristol Warsaw has been a meeting place for the artistic elites of Warsaw. A few personalities even lived at the hotel, including its founder, pianist and composer Ignacy Jan Paderewski. **Wojciech Fangor** was one of the most outstanding Polish artists of the twentieth century and the first from Poland to have a solo show dedicated to his work. He was deeply interested in celestial bodies and the cosmos, building his own optical devices and telescopes and even constructing his own observatory at his American estate. His op-art paintings include canvases with multicolored circles in which the colors blur into pulsating circular shadows, pulling in the viewer. These works are Fangor's interpretation of images of planets and stars as seen by inaccurate telescopes. He chose twenty-eight illustrations of constellations from astronomer Johannes Hevelius's atlas to magnify and paint over. One of them is his 1970 work *M64*, which is exhibited in Hotel Bristol's lobby. Guests love learning about Fangor's work in Warsaw and enjoy that he connects to the artistic environment of the hotel, where new art exhibitions are shown almost every month.

COLORED GLASS
IN COSTA SMERALDA

Hotel Cala di Volpe was built by architects **Jacques and Savin Couëlle** to resemble an ancient fishing village. This was in line with the vision of Prince Aga Khan, the destination's founder, to mimic the coastline and its rounded rock formations and let the architecture be part of the natural landscape. The Couëlles took a particularly artistic approach to their profession. The hotel's wine cellar, La Cave, and its main restaurant use colored glass that Jacques broke into pieces. In the restaurant, the glass was positioned at different angles in the wall, permitting the outside light to filter in from the corridors of the ground floor and mezzanine. In the wine cellar, this same decor gives the impression of a sanctuary, since the colored glass resembles church windows, allowing the space to act as a temple of art, wine, and hospitality for guests.

HOTEL DANIELI

VENICE, ITALY

THE PRIDE OF MURANO

In 1987, **Anzolo Fuga**, a master glassblower born into one of Murano's oldest and most distinguished glassblowing lineages, made a set of stained-glass panels for Hotel Danieli's Palazzo Dandolo that are a perfect example of Venetian craftsmanship. Fuga dedicated his professional life to the creation of stained-glass and leaded-glass panels, vases, and other glass objects and was the director of the Abate Zanetti School of Glass in Murano for more than twenty years. The three interlaced palaces that make up Hotel Danieli date back to the fourteenth century and house a rich collection of precious art and antiques, including precious fabrics, Murano glass chandeliers, and mirrors. Fuga's stained-glass panels represent the continuation of one of Venice's oldest crafts into the twentieth century. His work can also be seen in various churches and at Palazzo Barbarigo in Venice, in a synagogue in Jerusalem, and a distinctive chapel in southwestern Australia.

ABATE ZANETTI SCHOOL OF GLASS

Calle Briati, 8b - 30141 Venice, Italy
+39 041 273 7711
lascuoladelvetro.it

Open Monday–Friday
9 a.m.–1 p.m. and 2–6 p.m.

FORTY YEARS OF DESIGN IN PARIS

The Hotel de Berri feels like a personal residence with an art collection. In the restaurant, a fresco by Parisian painter **Hippolyte Romain** tells the story of the designers living in Paris in the twentieth century, most notably Elsa Schiaparelli, who lived at the address when it was a hôtel particulier. Romain's work was discovered by Anna Piaggi, former editor in chief of *Vanity*, who offered him fifteen pages in the avant-garde magazine for his illustrations of Milanese fashion. His style is ideal for the hotel's philosophy and spirit, since he has lived in Paris for decades and observed his subjects firsthand. His drawings and paintings show more details than a photograph: He includes inimitable emotion in his artful documentation of these designers. With its singular style, Romain's work even gives an idea of the future and what could come next in the world of fashion design.

SOFÍA SANCHEZ DE BETAK
art director and fashion consultant

DO YOU HAVE A FAVORITE ITEM OR COLLECTIBLE THAT YOU
ALWAYS SEEK OUT WHEN TRAVELING?

I generally fall for the local craft, whether it's sandals, carpets, or wine. It depends on the destination, though I think the common denominator in most trips is vintage jewelry.

WHY DO YOU LIKE TO COLLECT THESE ITEMS FROM YOUR TRAVELS?

They tell a story of the country's past and their people, and they preserve well through time.

DO YOU HAVE ANY FAVORITE LOCAL MEMENTOS THAT YOU HAVE COLLECTED
FROM YOUR TRAVELS? WHY ARE THEY SPECIAL? WHERE ARE THEY FROM?

My engagement ring, from the Grand Bazaar in Istanbul.

HOW DO YOU LIKE TO CURATE, ORGANIZE, OR DISPLAY KEEPSAKES
FROM YOUR TRAVELS AT HOME?

In my jewelry box—and by wearing them, of course!

IS THERE SOMETHING THAT YOU HAVE COVETED FROM A HOTEL OR A HOTEL ROOM?

Stationery. I love it when hotels print your name on their letterhead. It makes me want to write letters.

WHAT ARE YOUR TIPS FOR TRAVELERS WHO WANT TO BRING HOME
A UNIQUE AND AUTHENTIC SOUVENIR?

Look for what the area specializes in, whether it's leather, weaving, jewelry, or embroidering.

HOTEL DES INDES

THE HAGUE, NETHERLANDS

LIGHTING
A PALATIAL LOUNGE

Hotel Des Indes underwent a stunning 35 million euro renovation in 2006, during which designer Jacques Garcia restored and even improved upon its original magnificence. This refurbishment included rich jewel tones and luxurious fabrics, but a major highlight is the beautiful chandelier that crowns the Des Indes Lounge & Terrace. Created in 1858, the beautiful fixture was originally designed to run on gas, as evidenced by its built-in taps, which would have been used to adjust the luminosity.

THE SAMOVAR: HONORING RUSSIAN ROOTS

A samovar is a decorative urn made from copper or silver that can hold a large quantity of water. Traditionally, its inside chamber was heated with coals to keep the water hot and bubbling all day long so that tea could be prepared at a moment's notice. The first officially documented Russian samovars were made in Tula in 1778 by brothers Ivan and Nazar Lisitsyn. Their small workshop was founded by their father, Fyodor Lisitsyn, a gunsmith. Fyodor experimented with creating samovars in various shapes, including barrels, engraved vases, and eggs; they often featured dolphin-shaped taps or loop-shaped handles. In the past, the samovar was not only a symbol of a cozy home but also a sign of a family's prosperity. Samovars could be found in all echelons of Russian society, from the imperial court to a peasant's hut. In modern Russia, samovars are rarely used to boil water for tea as originally intended, but many families place them in the center of the table during holiday celebrations. Reserving pride of place for a samovar at the festive table is both a tribute to Russian ancestors and an embodiment of warmhearted hospitality. At Hotel National, samovars made in Tula are used in the breakfast room and at Bar Alexandrovsky, the perfect touch to show that the hotel values excellent service.

HOTEL FUERSTENHOF
LEIPZIG, GERMANY

A BLÜTHNER IN THE PIANO BAR

Leipzig, with its proximity to Paris, London, and Vienna, is a pillar of European musical culture. When **Julius Blüthner** founded his piano company there in 1853, his instruments were quickly recognized for their outstanding technical qualities and were established in concert halls all over the world. Hotel Fürstenhof has always been linked to Leipzig's musical history, playing host to musical performances as well as exclusive exhibitions and literature readings. The Blüthner piano in the hotel bar, thought to have been crafted around 1912, embodies this tradition. During the winter, concerts by local musicians allow guests to take a nostalgic journey back in time to the world of nineteenth-century salon music. To this day, the Blüthner family of craftsmen continues to personally oversee the production of each instrument bearing their name. A Blüthner piano requires nearly a year to complete, from the first cut of the saw to the final tuning and polishing. The heart of the instrument is its resonating soundboard, specially crafted from 150-year-old spruce trees from the Austrian Alps. Each piano also boasts layers of lacquer polished to a perfect mirror shine and accents of exotic wood veneer such as African Bubinga or bird's-eye maple to line its inner case.

DESIGNING A DIRNDL

In 2015, Hotel Goldener Hirsch and local clothing designer **Susanne Spatt** created a dirndl, or traditional Austrian dress, for the hotel. It was an exclusive design, and 10 percent of the profits went to UNICEF. Now, the signature Goldener Hirsch dirndl is a yearly collaborative project, with a new design each time. To make the dirndl, Spatt prints her fabrics by hand in the hotel's colors: pink, light blue, green, yellow, and red. She gives each piece careful attention, adding charming details such as colorful buttonholes, glittering Swarovski crystals, noble mink, silk ribbons, and ruffles. Once completed, the design is exhibited in the hotel lobby for visitors to admire and is available for purchase at Spatt's Salzburg shop. The dirndl is worn at folk festivals, on festive occasions, at parties, or even as an everyday dress, and it is included in the traditional outfits still worn by Hotel Goldener Hirsch's staff. Spatt's designs ensure that this clothing will not only survive but thrive.

SUSANNE SPATT SHOP

Aigner Straße 32
5026 Salzburg
+43 662 874452 30
susanne-spatt.com

A BEADED BLESSING

Worry beads, called *kombolói*, are a traditional element of Greek culture. Each string of beads consists of thirty-three local precious or semiprecious stones that users can manipulate with one or two hands, making time pass easily and bringing a moment of relaxation and peace. This curious object was first depicted in a 3,500-year-old Minoan-era fresco found at the Akrotiri archaeological site in Santorini. The creation of a string of worry beads begins with the gathering of the silver, gold, or alloy elements that will become the beads. These can come from markets or antiques stores, or be crafted by the artist. **Yiannis Aggelakis**, the artisan who created the many *kombológia* available in Hotel Grande Bretagne's gift shop, next visualizes whom the piece will appeal to, which helps him select the materials, colors, sizes, weights, values, and number of beads. One by one, Aggelakis checks, alters, and strings the beads. When they glide together, he listens to their sound and pays attention to the way they feel in his hands, ensuring everything feels right. Then the center stone, or *papas*, is fixed. The string symbolizes the never-ending nature of time, and the papas bead, often larger and more ornate, represents completion or ascension. The final touch is the *founda*, the elegant, silky tassel tied at the end of the string, behind the papas. And then the kombolói is complete and receives its good-luck blessing from the artist.

THE NYMPH OF THE DANUBE

According to Viennese legend, the Danube Nymph was a warmhearted woman who warned boatmen away from the rocks and rapids of the river Danube. Hotel Imperial chose this eye-catching sculpture depicting her, and it has been the jewel of its neo-Renaissance Royal Staircase ensemble for more than eighty years. The nymph was created by **Hans Gasser**, an Austrian sculptor also known for a work that portrays Empress Elizabeth "Sisi" in Vienna's Wien Westbahnhof train station. Gasser was a professor at the Academy of Fine Arts Vienna. His nymph statue completes the hotel's palatial atmosphere, which is also enhanced by a magnificent portrait of Emperor Franz Joseph I, by S. von Zaszer, that hangs above the Ceremonial Staircase.

THE BASQUE BERET

**SOMBRERERÍA
CASA PONSOL**

Narrika Kalea, 4
20003 San Sebastián
Gipuzkoa
Spain
+34 943 42 08 76
casaponsol.com

Open
Monday–Friday
10 a.m.–1 p.m.
and 4–8 p.m.
Saturday
10 a.m.–1:30 p.m.
and 4–8 p.m.

The *txapela*, or Basque-style beret, is a traditional garment representative of Basque culture. Berets were popularized throughout Europe, as reflected by the various translations of their name: *béret basque* in French, *Baskenmütze* in German, *basco* in Italian, and *baskeri* in Finnish. The hat's colors vary by region and purpose: black and blue are for more everyday wear, while red and white are reserved for festivities. At Hotel Maria Cristina, porters welcome guests while proudly wearing their *txapelas*. Guests love this sartorial touch and often ask to borrow the berets for photos. These hats, available at Sombrerería Casa Ponsol in San Sebastián, are made by artisans **Boinas Elósegui** in Tolosa. The shop, open since 1838, is the oldest in Basque Country and has dressed the heads of kings such as Alfonso XIII and musicians including Bruce Springsteen. Meanwhile, the manufacturer's artisans have been producing hats for 160 years and are the sole group with the passion to continue creating them in the traditional way.

THE WINES OF LA RIOJA

Marqués de Riscal is one of the oldest wineries in the Rioja region. Founded in Elciego in 1858 by Guillermo Hurtado de Amézaga, it has always been a point of reference for the winemaking business at both the national and international level, as well as a destination for millions of visitors from around the world. The **Bodegas de los Herederos del Marqués de Riscal** comprise an innovative, pioneering cellar that seeks to create original, fresh, elegant, and easy-to-drink wines. Of course, house wines are served in all of Hotel Marqués de Riscal's bars and restaurants and at many other Luxury Collection properties, but they can also be found for sale at other locations in 110 countries. Wine is integrated into the entire experience of a stay at the hotel. When guests check in, a bottle of Rioja awaits them in their rooms. The winery tour shows off the Cathedral cellar, where each year's prize wines are kept. Even the spa is dedicated to wines: Guests can choose from distinctively luxurious treatments, including a wine-barrel bath, a crushed cabernet scrub, a honey-and-wine wrap, and a grape facial treatment.

HOTEL PITRIZZA
PORTO CERVO, ITALY

WEAVING WITH THE SARDINIAN LANDSCAPE

Hotel Pitrizza was conceived to meld with the environment that surrounds it. Architect Luigi Vietti defined the perfect fusion between nature and architecture and between tradition and innovation, striving to use only basic, natural shapes in his designs. Thus, all of the property's roofs are covered with authentic grass for camouflage, disguising the pink granite buildings among the fragrant juniper. The first infinity pool in the history of hospitality was built here, creating a man-made place to swim that appeared to reach back into its surroundings. Making handmade woven baskets is part of ancient Sardinian tradition, still alive thanks to the dedication of local artisans who preserve the craft, handing it down over the generations. A Sardinian basket weaver uses dried local plants such as asphodel, reeds, dwarf palms, straw, and myrtle wood. These materials are ideal on account of their flexibility. In Sardinia, baskets are common gifts, and are hung on walls and used for domestic or decorative purposes. Hotel Pitrizza's baskets, which are placed in the property's newest villas and suites, were made with colors that fit perfectly with the surrounding design and natural landscape.

REPURPOSING NATURE AS ART

Hotel President Wilson, surrounded by the Quai Wilson promenade, Lake Geneva, and the Alps, uses three main themes in its design: water, light, and the nearby landscape. The work of Korean artist **Jae Hyo Lee** helps emphasize these elements. First, the hotel's main entry shows off a ceiling shaped like a water drop covered in white-gold leaf. Beneath, another of Lee's pieces calls to mind an object falling on a sheet of water, its curved screens made of metal mesh creating Chinese shadow effects. A platinum mosaic wall with wave motifs completes the scene. And in the Glow Bar, a stylized white-lacquer wave ceiling reflects the changing mood of the nearby lake, while two more of Lee's works evoke water droplets bursting in suspension. Lee creates his pieces mainly with natural materials found near his home. A pebble, a branch, or a fallen tree could be a starting point. He uses a recycling approach to give things another life, honoring the materials he finds by respecting their natural shapes and using their original forms as guidance for the art they will ultimately become. Lee stresses the impact of humans on nature, encouraging people to appreciate the richness and beauty of what surrounds them.

SCHLOSS FUSCHL
HOF BEI SALZBURG, AUSTRIA

THE SETTING FOR *SISSI*

In the 1950s, Schloss Fuschl was used as the set for the film *Sissi* and its two sequels, starring Romy Schneider as Empress Elisabeth of Austria. The hotel stands in for Possenhofen Castle on Lake Starnberg, Elisabeth's childhood home, which symbolized her carefree youth. The well-appointed Sissi Suite celebrates Schloss Fuschl's role in these films with its breathtaking view over Lake Fuschl, and unique pieces from Empress Elisabeth's estate, as well as scenes from the films, are on view in the hotel's Sissi Museum. The exhibition includes photographs of the royal family's daily life, as well as rare pieces from the empress's personal collection, such as a medallion and locket owned by King Ludwig II of Bavaria. After the king's death in 1886, his mother gave the medallion to his close confidante, Empress Elisabeth, in memory of her son.

KING GEORGE

ATHENS, GREECE

THE CHANGING
OF THE HELLENIC GUARD

King George is situated just opposite Syntagma Square and the Greek Parliament, where every day two Evzones, also known as Tsoliádes, guard the Tomb of the Unknown Soldier. These Evzones are men selected exclusively from the Hellenic Army, and they have been symbols of Greek bravery and courage since 1868. During Sunday morning's Changing of the Guard, which takes place at eleven o'clock, each soldier must stand still, on duty, for sixty minutes, only moving when it is time to switch places with his colleague. Throughout the changing, the Evzones work in pairs to perfectly coordinate their movements, and it is a spectacle that Athenians and visitors alike gather to behold. Artist **Lisa Pentheroudaki** designed wooden versions of the Evzones to guard the lobby of King George, creating symmetry with the real-life Evzones it faces. Pentheroudaki elevated the significance of Evzones to a whole new level by embracing two strong elements of Greek heritage: the history of these soldiers and the purity of the beechwood she used to depict them, which is local to Athens.

LUGAL

ANKARA, TURKEY

THE ARTS OF ANATOLIA

Ankara is located at the center of the Anatolian peninsula, a land that has historically been at the crossroads of many civilizations. The region's history goes back to the Hattian civilization of the Bronze Age, as early as 2300 BC, followed by the Hittites in the second millennium BC, the Phrygians in the tenth century BC, and then the Lydians and Persians. The city subsequently fell to the Romans and then to the Byzantines. Sultan Alp Arslan of Great Seljuk opened the door into Anatolia for the Turks at the Battle of Manzikert in 1071. During the Ottoman Empire, the area was an important point on the caravan trade route to the east. By the nineteenth century, it had declined in importance, but it became prominent again when Mustafa Kemal Atatürk, former president of Turkey, chose it as the base from which to direct the Turkish War of Independence in 1919. Due to its role in the war and its strategic position, Ankara was declared the capital of the Republic of Turkey on October 13, 1923.

To celebrate Ankara's heritage and pay respect to all that made the city an important landmark over the centuries, Lugal worked with **Novarte**, a group of four illustrators led by Deniz Karagül, as well as the Museum of Anatolian Civilizations, to create a series of four artworks. The artists combined metal, ceramic, bronze, and oil painting on canvas, merging the elements of many civilizations to create products whose golden-brown hues match the hotel's color scheme. The works hang in Aruni Restoran & Bar, whose name means "meal" in the Hittite language.

METROPOL PALACE
BELGRADE, SERBIA

A SYMPHONY OF STAINED GLASS

As a building safeguarded by the Institute for the Protection of Cultural Monuments, the Metropol Palace's basic form has never changed despite numerous renovations. One of the best examples of this preservation, which highlights a historical aspect of the previous hotel, is the stained-glass artwork on the facade facing Kralja Aleksandra Boulevard, which is shown in its original position. The monumental stained-glass piece, named *Yugoslavian Symphony, devoted to nations and nationalities*, was made by renowned Serbian artisan **Stevan Stanišić** in 1957 with the help of famous professor and painter Vaso Pomorišac. It took six months to create the thirty-five-piece work, which is twenty-six feet high and sixteen feet wide and was the first art piece made in the style of Socialist realism. Stanisic's studio completed a full restoration of the piece in 2016.

MYSTIQUE

SANTORINI, GREECE

GIVING DRIFTWOOD A NEW LIFE

Designer **Frank Lefebvre** of Bleu Nature has a passion for breathing new life into driftwood, combining it with other natural materials, such as pebbles and lacquered wood, and bringing nature to modern interiors. He did just that for Mystique's tables, lamps, mirrors, and various other pieces found in the hotel's suites and villas. Lefebvre's effervescent style, brimming with youthful energy, harmonizes traditional architecture and cutting-edge technology. Every year, Bleu Nature's team combs beaches for driftwood. Large or small, straight or twisted, each piece deserves special attention. This wood needs no further processing because the water has frozen it in time. It is a perfect decor element for Mystique, a hotel carved into the rugged caldera cliffs and outfitted with lovingly handcrafted organic materials for minimalist elegance.

THE PARK TOWER KNIGHTSBRIDGE

LONDON, UNITED KINGDOM

A SIGNATURE HOTEL SCENT

The Park Tower Knightsbridge boasts a signature fragrance in the form of custom-made candles by **Rachel Vosper**. The hotel's scent was inspired by the flowers growing in Hyde Park, as well as the magnolia-blossom walls and stunning regal decor of the Knightsbridge Lounge. The hotel was thrilled to have the opportunity to collaborate with a local business situated within walking distance, allowing guests to not only enjoy the candles' scent from diffusers placed in the hotel suites but also to visit the artisan's shop. Guests may also book a candle-making workshop with the concierge.

**RACHEL VOSPER
CANDLE STORE**

69 Kinnerton Street - Belgravia
London SW1X 8ED
United Kingdom
+44 20 7235 9666
rachelvosper.com

Open Monday–Saturday
10 a.m.–6 p.m.

MAYFAIR FASHIONS OF THE TWENTIETH CENTURY

The Westbury incorporates Mayfair, a historically high-end district of London, into its decor with a look back in time at the local fashions. A carefully curated selection of 190 black-and-white photos from 1910 to 1970 showcases female and male models throughout decades of style trends, in addition to demonstrating the evolution of photo techniques. The images, only accessible for guests to view, are featured along the hallways of the hotel's seven floors, with each floor chronicling a single decade. The Westbury Mayfair's owners, the Cola family, and the hotel's interior designer, Alex Kravetz, have collected these photos from various local auction houses and art galleries in Mayfair over the years. Not only do the images establish Mayfair as the trendsetter for prestigious fashion houses, new acquisitions also support the area's art scene.

LEFKARA LACE

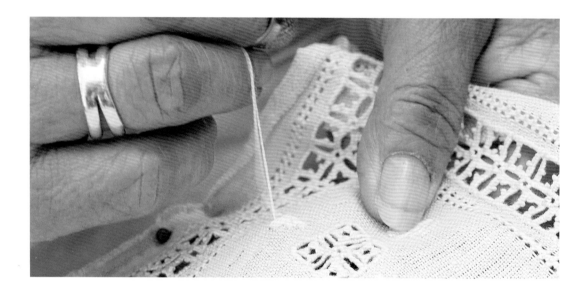

At Parklane, guests will notice an element that conveys the essence of local Cypriot identity, superior artistry, and exclusive luxury all in one eloquent form. Lefkara lace, or *lefkaritika*, takes its name from the village where the most difficult and complex lace designs have been made for centuries. Lefkaritika derived from a local embroidery called *asproploumia*, an all-white geometric pattern in satin stitch combined with simple drawn thread work that women throughout Cyprus made as part of their dowries. In medieval times, Lefkara was the favorite summer retreat of the ruling Venetian families, who took up embroidery as a hobby and influenced the designs of the local women. Lefkara lace is made by counting fabric threads, which is the reason why most of the lace patterns are strictly geometric. The embroidery consists of both designs embroidered over the cloth using the satin stitch and designs made by cutting and drawing specific threads of the fabric. Most patterns are named after everyday objects, such as lantern, cross, fork, snail, daisy, basket, and eye. An important feature of Lefkara lace is the river, a cut-and-draw design in a zigzag shape that runs parallel to the fabric's outside edges and encloses triangular areas that are filled in with designs. With all of these components, a single item of lefkaritika can take months to complete. The hotel features stunning examples of the lace itself on its beds, as well as Lefkara lace–inspired patterns on hanging and bedside lights, wallpaper, mirrors, and the frosted glass on the walk-in shower. Guests can buy their own lace in the village of Lefkara, about half an hour away.

A PIECE OF OLD PORTUGAL

The corridors and outdoor areas of The Pine Cliffs Hotel are decorated with traditional Portuguese tiles, called *azulejos*, which depict old customs, habits, or professions from many regions of the country, such as a rosemary salesman in Lisbon or a fish salesman in Aveiro. The striking art pieces also form headboards in every guest room. These ceramic tiles are hand-painted, then fired in an extremely hot oven to vitrify. The *azulejos* at Pine Cliffs were made by artisans at **Fábrica de Cerâmica Constância**, a factory that dated back to 1836 but closed shortly after Pine Cliffs' grand opening in 1992, making them even more rare and special. Guests often observe that the hotel is like a museum preserving the work of this particular group of artisans.

PRINCE DE GALLES
PARIS, FRANCE

THE PRINCE OF WALES'S CHANDELIER

Bar Les Heures at Prince de Galles is home to the Lee Lee Chandelier, created by interior designer Bruno Borrione—who also worked on the hotel's La Scène restaurant—and Murano glass factory **Andromeda**. This majestic blown-glass and twenty-four-karat-gold light fixture is an elegantly modern take on the Roaring Twenties. The piece, which uses three distinct lighting systems, took eight months to create. The chandelier lights the entire bar area, and its bottom side is fixed with a mirror, catching guests' attention with the optical illusions that are created by its interaction with mirrors spread throughout the room. The focus on light also gives the bar a different atmosphere depending on whether one visits for breakfast, lunch, or dinner. It is said that during the 1376 Battle of Crécy, King Edward III handed the Prince of Wales three ostrich feathers as a token of courage. Upon his death, the prince was renamed the Black Prince for his heroism, and his badge, known as The Prince of Wales's Feathers, became a national emblem. Still treasured by his modern-day namesake, it is accompanied by the inscription *"Ich dien,"* meaning "I serve," a motto cherished by the Prince de Galles hotel. The badge has been subtly worked into much of the hotel's decor, including the Lee Lee Chandelier.

HARVESTING MESSINIA'S LIQUID GOLD

The Romanos embraces the olive harvest, an age-old tradition that has been part of the daily lives of the Messinia region's people for centuries and can only be learned firsthand. Olive oil, which Homer dubbed "liquid gold," is a gift of nature and holds great biological and pharmaceutical value. The human body can assimilate up to 98 percent of it, which helps to lower cholesterol. During the hotel's construction, 6,500 olive trees, along with many other indigenous trees, were preserved through an extensive onsite replanting program. Beginning in early autumn, guests can learn about the olive-harvesting process, the local varieties of olives, and the tree-planting projects in the region, as well as participate in an olive oil tasting session. At the olive groves, huge nets are unrolled under the trees to catch the falling treasures, and harvesters drag plastic rakes over the trees' leaves to separate out the olives. The fruits are then gathered from the ground and taken to a nearby olive press to have their oil extracted.

According to culinary experts, the extra-virgin olive oil of Messinia ranks among the finest in the world. The unique climatic conditions and morphology of the soil play a significant role in ensuring high quality and a unique taste. **Navarino Icons**, Costa Navarino's authentic food line inspired by the region's culinary history that The Romanos's olive harvest helps to create, uses strict quality-control guidelines to produce olive oil made from the Koroneiki variety of olive, which tastes excellent and has the highest nutritional value. Olives of the renowned Kalamon variety, meanwhile, are carefully gathered by hand from Costa Navarino's centuries-old trees, ripened by the sun, tempered by the air, cured in natural brine, and packed in Costa Navarino's own extra-virgin olive oil to provide antioxidants and anti-inflammatory nutrients to their consumers.

SCULPTING THE AEGEAN SEA

Built right on the Aegean, Santa Marina already enjoys a closeness with the sea. Corals are an integral part of that sea's vibrant beauty, and as each one is different and a work of art in itself, they translate easily into an element of interior design. It took a talented local Greek artisan to be able to sculpt a resin replica of something so delicate and natural, and to capture the miracle of its beauty. The coral sculptures, placed in glass boxes over the bed in each guest room, act as a symbol of the sea and couple with the Aegean view to offer complete serenity. Continuing the theme, the table lamps on each escritoire are also made of coral, and coral wall lights and doorknobs can also be found throughout the hotel.

WEAVING BULGARIAN HISTORY

Tapestry weaving emerged as a craft in Bulgaria in the seventeenth century. In the lobby and ballrooms of Sofia Hotel Balkan are authentic pieces of art that weavers created especially for the hotel in 1976. Chiprovtsi tapestries are characterized by their smooth, dense texture; their geometric patterns; and their harmonious balance of warm and cool tints, including yellow, brown, red, blue, and green. Socioeconomic changes in the Ottoman Empire caused decorative tapestries to thrive in terms of variety and number produced. Weavers borrowed from nature, depicting trees, stars, birds, animals, and flowers in stylized patterns. The color palette expanded to include white and purple, and the craft spread into other villages in the region, which began to borrow themes from one other. Typical patterns included the Vine, the Wreaths, the Cart, the Tsvekets (Flowers), Bird Nests, the Columns, the Great Hooks, the Wings, the Feathers, and the Four Eyes. The period from Balkan liberation from the Ottomans in 1913 to the present day is known as the ornamental period for Chiprovtsi tapestries. Lifestyle changes and increasing competition with imported tapestries and carpets have led to the use of larger palettes and patterns. Chemical dyes and designs from other countries have also been introduced. These works of art have entered the collections of numerous European museums, where their craftsmanship can be preserved.

TRUMP TURNBERRY

AYRSHIRE, SCOTLAND

NAUTICAL DECOR
AT TURNBERRY LIGHTHOUSE

Turnberry Lighthouse has been a fixture of the Ayrshire coast since 1873. Originally commissioned by the Northern Lighthouse Board to warn passing vessels away from nearby Bristo Rock, the lighthouse is the oldest man-made structure on the Turnberry property save for the remains of the thirteenth-century castle of Robert the Bruce that it marks. The lighthouse is home to a luxurious two-bedroom suite with breathtaking views across the Irish Sea to the Isle of Arran and beyond. The rooms are tastefully decorated in rich mahogany and gold leaf. To continue the nautical theme, a striking collection of wooden paddles adorns the lounge area.

THE SECRETS OF SANTORINIAN WINE

A *maggano* is a round, wooden tool with a lid, used before modern technology was available by Santorinian wineries to press harvested grapes. The term was only used in Santorini; in other regions of Greece, the same apparatus is called a *strofilia*. Three maggana decorate Alati, Vedema's signature restaurant, within the four-hundred-year-old winery's stone walls.

After the *vedema*, or grape harvest (the term the resort takes its name from), the fruits gathered were collected in large tanks called *patitiria*, which comes from the Greek word *pato*, or "to step on." Winemakers would step on the grapes in the patitiria to smash them and collect their juice, called moustos. The juice was placed in wooden barrels, but not all of it was released with only the weight of a man's steps, so the rest was collected by the maggano to avoid waste. The maggano had a hole at its bottom and gaps between the pieces of wood that made up its sides. When its lever was turned, its lid pressed the grapes and allowed the *moustos* to leak out of these openings. This juice, which had a stiffer taste due to some of the grapes' pulp being included, was then collected in basins and poured into the barrels with the juice from the patitiria. The amount of magganies (contents of the maggano) used would determine the quality of the wine.

THE CIGAR CONNOISSEUR'S HAVEN

The Wellesley's cigar lounge is an intimate, decadent space featuring an Art Deco design reflective of the 1920s, complete with a portrait of Winston Churchill painted directly onto tobacco leaves. Each cigar in the hotel's bespoke walk-in humidor is hand-rolled by a Cuban cigar roller. The humidor, which is one of the largest in Europe, showcases more than $2 million worth of the world's finest specimens. It was commissioned by Italian furniture experts DeART in conjunction with Fox Linton fabrics, and it features a laser-cut marble inlaid map of Cuba. **Giuseppe Ruo**, The Wellesley's director of food and beverage, travels to Cuba to make his personal cigar selections, ensuring that the hotel's offerings are of the highest quality.

A notable cigar in The Wellesley's collection is the Cohiba Behike 40th Anniversary, hand-rolled by Norma Fernández Sastre, the personal roller to former Cuban president Fidel Castro. The newest addition to the hotel's collection is the Cohiba 50th Anniversary Humidor, of which only fifty were made; the hotel owns number fifty. The Cohiba 50th Anniversary cigar is the most expensive in the world, with each selling for about $15,000.

THE ALPHABET AS ART

The Alexander fuses modern and ancient culture with a custom-made work of art depicting the Armenian alphabet, which was created by linguist Mesrop Mashtots in the year 405 AD. This unique design element, 19.6 feet long and 9.8 feet wide, created by wood-art designer **Yuri Vardanyan at Konviga**, the famous Belarusian wood factory, is the centerpiece of the hotel's conference room foyer. It depicts one of Armenia's most significant cultural accomplishments, proudly on display for visitors from other nations to view. The thirty-nine linked wooden letters, made of alderwood and spray-painted in gold, represent Armenian identity and bring a vintage component to the hotel's decor. The letter *A* uses a unique design to emblematize The Alexander.

JUNIPER, A WOOD
FOR ALL THE SENSES

Sardinian tradition dictates that nature's raw materials should be used as Nature herself would use them. Juniper is a plant native to Sardinia that local artisans turn into art. Hotel Romazzino's Bar Ginepro is named after the fragrant shrubs woven into its decor. In response to the design concept set out by Prince Karim Aga Khan, former owner of the hotel, architect **Michele Busiri Vici** shaped juniper wood into powerful, flowing, sculptural forms influenced by Arabic, Moroccan, and Mediterranean buildings. The juniper-wood floors pair with the whitewashed walls for a highly sophisticated look, and the wood's scent ensures that staying at Hotel Romazzino is a multisensory experience.

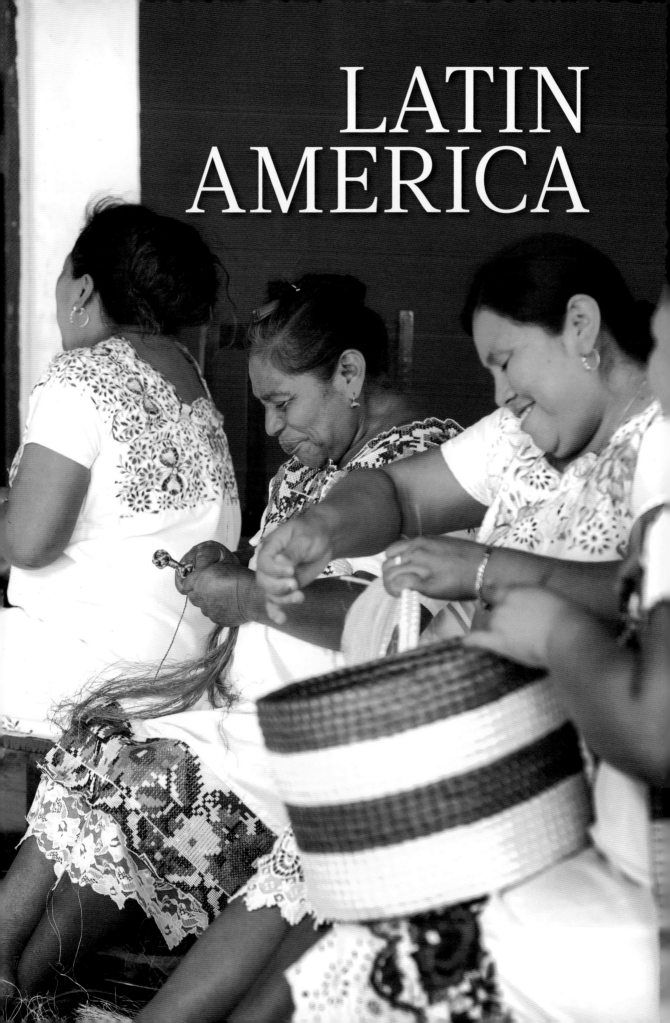

LATIN
AMERICA

THE BEST SIESTA IN CAMPECHE

At Hacienda Puerta Campeche and the four other Luxury Collection haciendas, hammocks are placed in the suites and at the pool. These cozy spaces are both a style element and a practical place to enjoy relaxation and rest. Hammocks are also the most-used bedding in the Yucatán Peninsula, so including them in the guest experience creates an authentic feel. Each hammock is made with a special device called a *bastidor*, which consists of two perpendicular poles separated from one another, about three to six feet apart. The distance between the poles depends on the hammock's size, and once this is set, the hammock thread is placed around the poles to form a skein. Then the poles can move toward one another, and the thread can interlace to form a net. The haciendas' hammocks are woven by artisans at the **Fundación Haciendas del Mundo Maya**, an organization that generates opportunities for socioeconomic development through handcraft workshops.

A SAINTLY CERAMIC FIGURE

The altar at Hacienda San Jose's chapel features an image of Saint Bonaventure as well as a figure of this iconic saint, who represents humbleness and a passion for service. Historical archives show that one day, the pope came to visit Saint Bonaventure in a small town near Florence to deliver him the special hat that cardinals wear, and he found him washing dishes for the community outside a convent. When the saint saw the pope, he said he wanted to finish his chore before receiving the hat, since he received great satisfaction from helping others. Thus, unlike other saints, who are usually depicted without hats, Saint Bonaventure is shown wearing the hat he received. Saint Bonaventure's values tie in closely with the hacienda's philosophy and passion for providing guests with an excellent stay. The hand-painted ceramic figure in the chapel has been passed down from generation to generation, and it is believed to have been created in the seventeenth century by local community members under the command of the Spanish priests from nearby churches.

HENEQUEN HANDCRAFTS

The henequen plant is an agave native to southern Mexico and Guatemala. Hacienda Santa Rosa used to process the fibers of this plant for use in crafts. Now, at the local workshops of the **Fundación Haciendas del Mundo Maya**, artisans take the rough fibers, which are usually green, and paint them. They then "comb" the fibers so they will be smoother and easier to braid and twist. There are different techniques depending on what the fibers are being used for, but most often they are knit together and shaped into coasters, keychains, bags, and baskets. The craft is present in many elements of the hotel, such as in the keychains for the room keys, the baskets in the rooms, and the coasters at the restaurant. Henequen products are also available in the hotel boutique and at local workshops. Rather than using synthetic fibers or other types of materials, Hacienda Santa Rosa has embraced its past and natural surroundings and delights in creating these products, working with local artisans and demonstrating its commitment to sustainable practices.

HACIENDA TEMOZON

TEMOZON SUR, YUCATÁN, MEXICO

COMFORTABLE IN
YUCATECAN COTTON

The huipil is a traditional Yucatecan dress popular as everyday wear for women. Huipils are typically made of cotton, so they are light and comfortable to wear even during hot days. They can feature bold colors all over or be plain with a decorative strip of colored flowers. Female staff members at Hacienda Temozon wear huipils hand-embroidered by local artisans at the workshops of the **Fundación Haciendas del Mundo Maya** as their work uniform. The garments are unique, as they are made to measure, and incorporate the richness of vegetation, flowers, and other natural elements found in the hacienda and in the surrounding community.

REFLECTING ON RESIN

The finish applied to Hacienda Uayamon's swimming pool and plunge pools, called chukum, comes from a natural wine-colored resin from the chukum tree, a species local to the Yucatán Peninsula and grown near the hacienda. Once combined with cement and left to set, chukum looks like natural stone, but when it reflects the sun, it makes the hacienda's pool water look turquoise, like the water found in the cenotes along the peninsula. The Mayans used chukum for cave paintings, mortars, stucco, and tanning and coloring skins. Nowadays, it is mainly used to coat walls, floors, furnishings, and pools, as an alternative to synthetic paints. It is preferred for pools due to its plasticity and setting properties, as it reduces cracking and increases impermeability, and it is also very smooth to the touch. Hacienda Uayamon's pools were finished by local artisans whose specialized knowledge has been passed down for generations. Each part of the process is done by hand, from the moment the chukum seed is planted to the extraction of the resin to the application of the resin mix. With their bright, clear, cenote-like waters, the hacienda's pools are the perfect complement to the pool area's seventeenth-century ruins.

WARIS AHLUWALIA

designer

DO YOU HAVE A FAVORITE ITEM OR COLLECTIBLE THAT YOU
ALWAYS SEEK OUT WHEN TRAVELING?

*There are two directions I'm drawn in—one is toward the history of a place
and the other is its celebration of craft. So it's either antiques or the work of local craftspeople.
Both have stories to tell; both provide insight into a culture. Treasures.*

WHY DO YOU LIKE TO COLLECT THESE ITEMS FROM YOUR TRAVELS?

*One of my favorite pieces is from the 1800s—a hand-painted poster with elements of collage.
It was purchased from an antiques dealer in the sixth arrondissement of Paris,
and it commemorates the siege of Rome by the French in the summer of 1849.*

DO YOU HAVE ANY FAVORITE LOCAL MEMENTOS THAT YOU HAVE COLLECTED
FROM YOUR TRAVELS? WHY ARE THEY SPECIAL? WHERE ARE THEY FROM?

They find their place somehow.

HOW DO YOU LIKE TO CURATE, ORGANIZE, OR DISPLAY KEEPSAKES
FROM YOUR TRAVELS AT HOME?

*Who doesn't covet an ashtray here and there, even us nonsmokers?
I always find a good use for them—not saying I've taken any.*

IS THERE SOMETHING THAT YOU HAVE COVETED FROM A HOTEL OR A HOTEL ROOM?

Stationery. I love it when hotels print your name on their letterhead. It makes me want to write letters.

WHAT ARE YOUR TIPS FOR TRAVELERS WHO WANT TO BRING HOME
A UNIQUE AND AUTHENTIC SOUVENIR?

Stay out of shopping malls. Walk the streets; spend time weaving your way through the city.

MAKING THE PERFECT PISCO

In the lobby of Hotel Paracas, guests will notice clay jugs, or *pisqueras*: the most identifying element of traditional pisco. These containers, in their original form, were used hundreds of years ago in Ica, Peru. In the mid-sixteenth century, the manufacturing industry for the *botija*, the drinking jug used for fermentation of the must that was used in the distillation of pisco brandy, was already flourishing, accompanying the expansion of the vineyards. Throughout the pisco production area, these jars became so important that they were even used as currency in commercial transactions.

THE LACQUERWARE OF OLINALÁ

The history of Mexican lacquerware traces back to pre-Hispanic times, when Olinalá, a city in the state of Guerrero, was known for the artisan pigments and dyes that were used to create the lacquered pieces. The Mexican technique arose independently of Asian lacquerware, but during the seventeenth and eighteenth centuries, it was influenced by trade with Asia. Olinalá lacquer artifacts are made with linaloe, a local wood with a particular herbal smell. Generally, the illustrations have nature themes, including flowers, foliage, landscapes, and animals, with a strong preference for the rabbit. For the aplicado technique, gold paint is applied with a very fine cat-hair paintbrush. For the rayado technique, the outline of an illustration is engraved, then the remaining lacquer is removed, leaving the design in relief. Each piece is then left to dry for several days before the last step: applying a linseed oil varnish. The anfitriones (butlers) at Las Alcobas use Olinalá trays created by local artisans to deliver items to guests, and lacquerware accessories are also incorporated throughout the hotel. The pieces are often the result of a collaboration of many individuals in artisan families, and no two pieces are the same.

LIVING INCA HISTORY

Palacio del Inka's stone wall, located between the hotel's foyer and restaurant, dates back to the Inca Empire in the sixteenth century. The Incas achieved deep spiritual and physical connections with nature. They built shrines and temples to worship their most important deities: the sun, the moon, and Pachamama, also known as Mother Earth. These buildings featured core stones, such as green diorite, which represented the union of the three spiritual realms: *hanaq pacha*, the upper realm that included the sun, moon, and stars; *kay pacha*, the perceptible world where humans, animals, and plants live; and *ukhu pacha*, the underworld, associated with the dead and new life.

Walls and buildings that had core stones embedded within them were considered to be alive, the stone having become the building's heart. If the stone was removed, the wall would crumble and "die." Guests of Palacio del Inka enjoy placing their hands on the stone wall to absorb its positive energy and can feel the heat from it flowing through their hands. To add to visitors' experience of Incan culture, the hotel also conducts an ancient ceremony at the wall to thank the earth, Pachamama, and the Incan *apus*, or mountain gods. This practice involves offering a *k'intu*, or a grouping of three coca leaves, symbolizing the three spiritual realms, to ask for protection, a good harvest, health, happiness, or money.

INTERWEAVING EUROPE
AND LATIN AMERICA

Known affectionately as the Paris of South America, Buenos Aires embraces and blends Europe's sophistication and Latin America's passion. In line with this cultural fusion, Park Tower's lobby showcases a beautiful Aubusson tapestry made in France in the nineteenth century. Purchased from a San Telmo antiques shop, the tapestry depicts a war in which Alexander the Great is giving honors to the family of Darius, the Persian emperor whom he has just defeated. The figures in the scene, along with the Chinese folding screens and other fine furniture pictured, give the impression of being in the living room of an aristocratic Argentinean palace in the early twentieth century.

SAN CRISTOBAL TOWER

SANTIAGO, CHILE

A CURATED VIEW OF THE ANDES

The views of the Andes from San Cristobal Tower are spectacular, especially in winter, when the mountains are pure white with snow. The observable vista also includes such landmarks as the Cordillera de Los Andes, the tallest building in South America, as well as the sunset reflected in the buildings, if one is looking at just the right time. The best way to enjoy the sight is with binoculars; some pairs are available at the hotel, at 21 Bar and Lounge, on the tower's twenty-first floor. The bar's delicious offerings, highlighting pisco and other Chilean specialties, complete this idyllic setting.

THE SANTA MARIA

PANAMA CITY, PANAMA

A SPIRITUAL FLOWER
TURNED TO GOLD

The Flower of the Holy Spirit is a type of orchid indigenous to Panama, chosen as the country's national flower because of its pristine beauty and spiritual symbolism: Its petals appear to form a tiny shrine in which a dove is resting, extending its wings to the world and wishing peace to mankind. A framed wax-casting work of art created by **Treasures of Panama by Reprosa** featured in The Santa Maria's lobby makes the flower look as if it has been turned to gold and silver. The leading company in the preservation and promotion of Panama's history, cultural traditions, ecological beauty, and ethnic diversity, Treasures of Panama has created pieces that have become objects of pride and admiration around the globe since 1975. Guests of the hotel are invited to visit the artisan's workshop, which is just minutes away, to observe the lost-wax casting process.

The Holy Spirit orchid blooms for less than two months of the year, so it is imperative to take advantage of the flower's short life span and choose the most perfect examples of its bud and bloom to create the type of casting shown in The Santa Maria's lobby. The individual parts of the plant are placed into a wax cylinder base and covered with wax investment. The cylinder is baked in an oven at 1,500°C for sixteen hours to burn away the elements of the plant, leaving only its impression behind. The impression is injected with sterling silver by means of centrifugal casting, or lost-wax casting. The hot cylinder is then doused in water to break the investment away, leaving the silver castings. These pieces are clipped away from the base and hand-worked to expose the beautiful elements of the flower. Some of the pieces are electroplated in twenty-four-karat gold to contrast with the silver, allowing the petals to reveal the tiny dove inside the bloom.

REPROSA COSA DEL ESTE

Parque Industrial, Calle Primera
Costa del Este
Panama
+507 271 0033
treasuresofpanama.com

Open Monday–Friday
8 a.m.–4:30 p.m.
Saturday
7 a.m.–3 p.m.

CELEBRATING
COLLECTIVE INTELLIGENCE

Renowned Mexican artist **César López-Negrete** spent years traveling to various regions of the Baja California Peninsula and studying its history, people, landscape, traditions, and art. One of his signature pieces is *Collective Intelligence*, a 10.5-by-7-foot intaglio mural on brass and patina. Fittingly located at Solaz's waterfront Al Pairo restaurant, the work depicts a school of jackfish swimming through the northernmost reef in Cabo Pulmo, a protected 27.5-square-mile marine area estimated to be 20,000 years old. John Steinbeck wrote about these reefs, their teeming life, and their electric colors in his 1951 book *The Log from the Sea of Cortez*. Cabo Pulmo was once heavily fished, but the local fishermen, particularly more recent generations of the Castro family, realized that they had to give up their profession to protect the ecosystem, and one by one, every species of sea creature has returned. It is now a popular diving area and even a habitat to some endangered species. López-Negrete's mural celebrates the collective intelligence between the fish and the fishermen who ensure their survival. The sculpture's engraved brass plates were created using the intaglio technique. The process uses acid to corrode an imprint in the metal and, through the use of various chemicals and oils at different temperatures, the work plays with depth, shadow, and light, producing a spectrum of hues.

THE QUIPU'S CULTURAL TIES

The word *quipu* comes from the Quechua word *khipu*, which means "knot." A quipu is made using various colorful wool or cotton ropes. It was invented by Andean civilizations and was widely used as an accounting system by *quipucamayocs (khipu kamayuqkuna)*, administrators of the Inca Empire, to collect data and keep records. Some historians have proposed that the quipu could also have been used as a graphic writing system. A quipu consists of a main rope onto which other ropes are knotted. Each rope has a different color, shape, and size. The colors identify different sectors, and the knots represent quantities in a base ten positional system. They range in size and complexity from very simple ones with a few strings to others with up to two thousand strings. Zero is normally represented by the absence of a knot in the proper position. Tambo del Inka's quipus were made by local artisans at **Sumaqkay**, and they are featured in the hotel's lobby, corridors, and guest rooms so that guests may view them and try their hand at interpreting the wealth of information they convey.

SUMAQKAY

Galería Arequipa
Jirón Alexander Von Humboldt 1527
La Victoria 15018 | Peru
+51 1 2646777
sumaqkayparacas.com

Open Monday–Saturday
10 a.m.–8 p.m.
Sunday 10 a.m.–6 p.m.

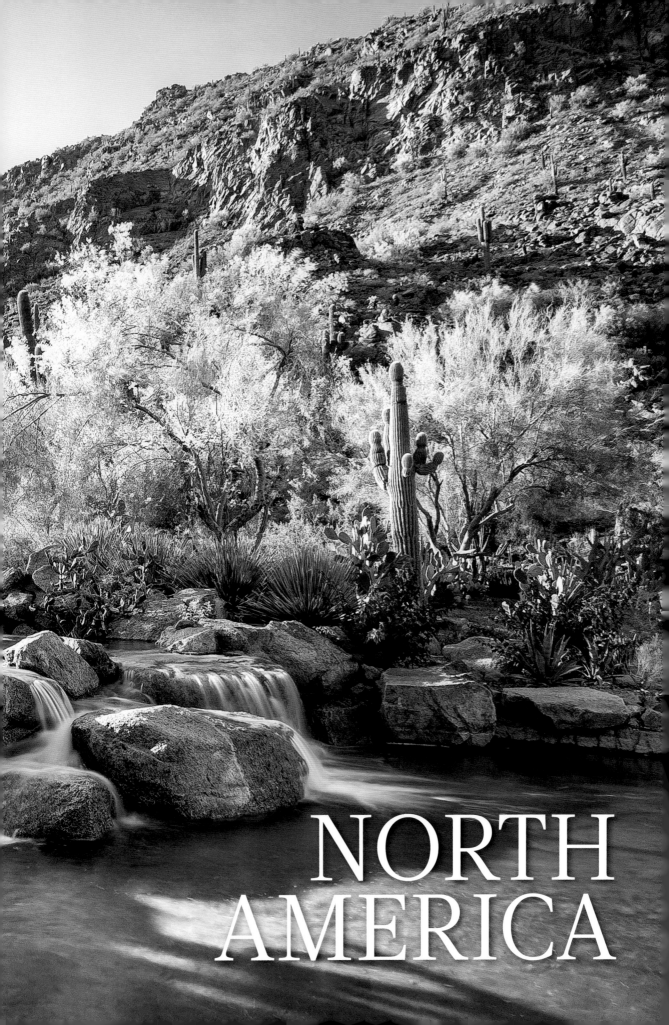

NORTH
AMERICA

THE BALLANTYNE
CHARLOTTE, NORTH CAROLINA, USA

LAVENDER LIVING

Lavender has been used since ancient times to relieve tension and stress while also healing and uplifting the body and soul. To create an experience for guests to relax in a way that is unique to the Carolinas, The Ballantyne's spa offers the Carolina Lavender Collection. This signature collection captures what makes the Carolinas special. Each treatment features a custom blend celebrating local lavender fields. The blend is made in small batches and sourced from the best ingredients to help aid deep relaxing and nurturing. Guests appreciate the locally inspired take on this popular and well-loved ingredient with its natural healing effects.

SCULPTING THE SONORAN DESERT

The wave sculpture by local Arizona artist **Kerry Vesper** displayed in the lobby of The Canyon Suites plays to the textures and colors of the Sonoran Desert's natural landscape. Inspired by forms with movement that he sees in nature, Vesper uses wood to capture the essence of a flying flag, flowing water, or molten glass. By gluing together layers of Baltic birch and colorful exotic wood, he builds pieces that appear bent. The wave's color and composition envelop the viewer, offering a tranquil, calming effect similar to the restorative influence of the warm desert, and striated layers of wood mimic the sedimentary rock of the landscape. The piece is defined by a richness that reinforces the hotel's overall design narrative, bringing the property a distinction all its own.

THE CHATWAL

NEW YORK, NEW YORK, USA

EMPIRE STATE ART DECO

Originally the home of America's first theatrical society, The Lambs Club—today The Chatwal—was designed by iconic architect and club member Stanford White, who also created the Villard Houses, the Washington Square Arch, and the original Madison Square Garden. Completed in 1905 and enlarged in 1915, the Lambs Club building served as the center of theater and entertainment in the city. The New York City Landmarks Preservation Commission stipulated that both its facade and many of its interior design elements had to be retained in The Chatwal, conditions that architect Thierry Despont and his team used to great effect. To hark back to the club's heyday, Despont used the timeless glamour of 1930s Art Deco as inspiration. The hotel bar, and specifically its Empire State Building–shaped lighting fixture, blurs the divide between classic and modern to create an intimate atmosphere.

THE GWEN'S CREATIVE MUSE

When Chicago's McGraw-Hill building was first constructed in 1928, stone bas-relief zodiac sculptures by Chicago-born artist **Gwen Lux**, from whom The Gwen takes its name, adorned its side. Today, replicas of these sculptures are featured on panels in the hotel's lobby, and custom murals of the works can be found above the headboard in each guest bedroom. The original pieces are located in the main lobby of the Shops at North Bridge, near the hotel. Each iteration of Lux's work brings the spirit of Art Deco to Chicago's Magnificent Mile, evoking the golden era of luxury on Michigan Avenue and raising the artist, one of few women in her field at the time, to prominence.

MAKING THE MOST OF VERMONT'S MAPLES

Vermont is known for its maple syrup, and there's nothing like the real thing. Generally, the maple tree sap season is between mid-February and mid-March, or when the temperature rises above freezing during the day and falls below freezing at night. The rising temperature creates pressure in the tree and generates the sap flow. To tap a tree, the sap collector drills a hole about three feet from the ground, ideally above a large root or below a large branch on the tree's south side. The hole is angled upward to facilitate the flow of sap. A spile, or small spigot, is then inserted, and a bucket is hung below it to collect the sap. The Equinox relies on local farms, such as Taylor Farm and **Dutton Farm**, for the best maple syrup Vermont has to offer. Guests can visit these farms for tastings and to learn about the tapping process. Daniel Black, the hotel's executive chef, makes a number of maple-centric dishes, such as black kale salad with cured maple bacon and smoked maple vinaigrette, charcuterie with maple apple butter, and maple bread pudding. Marsh Tavern, the hotel restaurant, also serves maple beverages.

DUTTON BERRY FARM

Routes 11–30
Manchester, VT
United States
+1 802 362 3083
duttonberryfarm.com

Open Monday–Sunday
9 a.m.–7 p.m.

A LOOK BACK THROUGH MINNEAPOLIS'S HISTORY

When reimagining the event spaces on Hotel Ivy's third floor, the design team combined the histories of the local area and the building itself. Ten images, taken in the summer of 2016 and framed by Hennes Art Company, are placed throughout the skyway entrance, showing the city of Minneapolis through the lens of photographer **Nick Kelsh**. The photos show the integration of old and new in the Minneapolis landscape, a dynamic that mirrors the story of the Ivy Tower, which began as a humble potential cornerstone of a larger church and later received a historic designation and was included in the modern Hotel Ivy. Highlights include the historic Gold Medal Flour building, Minneapolis City Hall, the Walker Art Center, the Stone Arch Bridge, the First Avenue club, and the Mary Tyler Moore statue.

FLY-FISHING AS AN ART

Hotel Talisa's private dining room wall boasts an unconventional display: a collection of antique fishing reels. Sourced by DAC Art Consulting, the diverse yet cohesive collection of reels highlights the local attraction of Vail, Colorado—fly-fishing—and provides an unexpected history lesson by displaying a timeline of styles, materials, and designs. For example, reels were originally made of wood, but this was easily worn by use and the elements. Later models make use of more resistant materials such as Bakelite and lightweight metals. The artisans who made these reels were experts in their field, so that after the reels' lives out on the water, they are easily transformed into artwork.

LAS ALCOBAS

ST. HELENA, CALIFORNIA, USA

A JOURNEY THROUGH
THE HISTORY OF HEALING

Atrio, the spa at Las Alcobas, introduces guests to a two-and-a-half-hour tactile history of massage that draws from five thousand years of Chinese, Indonesian, Egyptian, and Indian healing traditions. The experience, created with **Marjorie Charlton** at Charlton Spa Concepts, builds on the philosophy of going backward to move forward, or resurrecting ancient techniques to gain new insights.

The Atrio Experience begins with a personalized aromatherapy blending. Guests co-create their own organic massage oil, of which they will take a bottle home, based on therapeutic objectives and scent palate. The first destination is China. The Tui Na massage, said to be the grandmother of all other techniques, is an oil-free rhythmic massage with a combination of acupressure, rolling, and rocking, increasing energy flow. Next along the journey is Egypt, where the massage therapist practices foot reflexology, the stimulation of organs through points on the foot. This also increases energy flow and releases stubborn blocks within the body. The experience continues to Indonesia, where a deep, flowing Balinese massage relieves and repairs muscles by smoothing and lengthening. Then in India, the home of five-thousand-year-old Ayurvedic medicine, guests undergo a Shirodhara treatment for ailments of the mind, mental stress, and migraines. Warm oil is poured steadily onto the forehead, allowing the brow muscles to release and encouraging the mind to let go. The final stop is an Indian scalp massage for deep relaxation, and the journey is complete.

FROM LOCKUP TO LIBERTY

The Liberty is the imaginative transformation of the storied Charles Street Jail—constructed between 1848 and 1851 by architect Gridley J. F. Bryant—into a luxury hotel. The jail, a cruciform granite building, was once home to some of Boston's legendary inmates, including former Boston mayor James Michael Curley and Frank Abagnale, Jr. The oculus windows, in the hotel's ninety-foot rotunda lobby, are original to the jail and provide natural light throughout the space. Four wrought-iron chandeliers, created by **Alexandra Champalimaud of Champalimaud Design**, mimic the shape of the windows, complementing the original structure already in place and preserving the spirit of this grittier side of Boston's history.

A CHANDELIER WITH A SONG

A focal point of the lobby at The Nines is *Bird Song*, a chandelier created by artist **Melody Owen**. The work is part of a collection of more than four hundred pieces of art commissioned by the hotel. Owen's thirty-foot work, composed of handblown glass spheres fabricated by Ian Gilula at Elements Glass, is a three-dimensional model of sound waves, specifically the songs of endangered birds indigenous to the Pacific Northwest. Illuminated from within by LED lights and strung together like necklaces, the "song" strands cascade downward like elegant blue beads. The choice of glass as a material conceptually echoes the fragile existence of birds and their songs.

THE PIED PIPER

PALACE HOTEL

SAN FRANCISCO, CALIFORNIA, USA

PAINTING THE PIED PIPER

The Pied Piper of Hamelin, an original painting by neoclassical artist **Maxfield Parrish**, is the pride of The Palace's Pied Piper bar. The work was commissioned specifically for the hotel's grand reopening in 1909 and depicts the Pied Piper leading citizens out of the town of Hamelin, Germany. It features twenty-seven unique expressive faces, including those of Parrish's wife, mistress, and two sons, and Parrish himself as the Pied Piper. The painting underwent a much-needed restoration in 2013, and when it was rehung in the bar, citizens of San Francisco flocked to see the new details the restoration had unveiled. In celebration, the mayor declared the day Pied Piper Day, and today the painting is valued at an estimated $4 million.

66 The Pied Piper Bar is not just a historic establishment—it is truly a San Francisco legacy. Maxfield Parrish's magical painting graces the room where millions of people have gathered to share stories, enjoy a great cocktail, and celebrate the spirit of our city. 99

MIKE BUHLER
president, San Francisco Heritage

THE STORY
OF A SOUTHERN BELLE

Drawing inspiration from its location in the heart of Savannah, Perry Lane Hotel chose artwork for its library to represent a contemporary take on a Southern belle's debutante portrait. *Flora*, an oil-on-canvas painting by New York artist **Deborah Brown**, fits into the narrative of Perry Lane Hotel's muse, Adelaide Harcourt, a fictional persona created by the hotel's curatorial team. A seventh-generation Savannian, Adelaide comes from a long line of financiers with a penchant for collecting. As the sole living Harcourt, she has made the arts community her family and Perry Lane Hotel her legacy gift to the city of Savannah, her one true love. She has traveled the globe, from New York to Paris to Istanbul, collecting art along the way. A former modern dancer who is passionate about literature and visual art, Adelaide has a genuine warmth and hospitality that make everyone feel at home, just like Perry Lane Hotel.

MONKEYING AROUND BEVERLY HILLS

Philippe Starck, the visionary designer behind SLS Hotel, wanted to infuse the property with an element of playfulness and sophisticated fun, something to remind guests to not take themselves too seriously. Monkeys were chosen as a design motif for their whimsicality, mischievousness, and energy, and they are woven throughout the hotel and the SLS crest. Starck tapped the digital artisans of London's **GBH (Gregory Bonner Hale) studio** to add their expertise to the project. The most famous and well-recognized examples of the theme are the morphing monkey videos shown nightly in The Bazaar by José Andrés: "The Dandy," "The General," "The Musician," "The Novelist," "The Royalist," "The Scientist," and "The Taxidermist." Each video shows a human figure transforming into a monkey still dressed in a regal suit. Monkey portraits can also be found outside of the hotel's meeting rooms, with each room named after a famous monkey from history and literature, including Albert, Clyde, Cornelius, Gordo, George, and Louie. Guests who want to take a bit of the SLS spirit home can purchase a bust of the General monkey from the video at the gift shop, Regalo.

A PLACE IN THE SUN

Solaris, a bronze-finished sculpture by **Seong-gu Lee**, sits atop an ebony elliptical base in The Phoenician's lobby. The work represents turning one's spirit to the sun for warmth and comfort. Its name, meaning "of the sun," is derived from Latin and speaks to Arizona's Sonoran Desert and the hotel's place within it. The artist's method was welding, but he wanted to go beyond the welding torch's manual instructions to experiment, instead of adhering to standardized rules and limitations. Thus, the torch became the artist's other hand, actually working as various tools that could melt, pare, adhere, scrape off, and color-coat. Lee's piece exudes an uplifting, inspiring spirit that encourages guests to surrender to the warmth and beauty of the surrounding landscape and enjoy the rejuvenating and carefree stay to come.

❝ *Solaris* captures the essence of The Phoenician's three-year transformation, providing guests with a new sense of being. Its soothing, emotional presence creates a welcoming feeling of release upon arrival. ❞

MARK VINCIGUERRA
general manager, The Phoenician

THE ROYAL HAWAIIAN
WAIKIKI, HAWAII, USA

LAUHALA: FROM GENERATION TO GENERATION

The hala tree is one of the most important plants to the Hawaiian people, and the craft of weaving lauhala, or *lau* (leaves) of the hala, has been passed down for generations. While the fruit of the tree is used as a food source on many Pacific islands and the trunk can be used as building material, the leaves are favored for weaving due to their softness, durability, and beauty. The Royal Hawaiian, surrounded by lush greenery, was once owned by Hawaiian royalty and is an ideal setting for gathering leaves for weaving. The hotel holds classes to teach guests how to make their own lauhala bracelets using traditional techniques. Expert *kumu* (teacher) **Ruby Hodges**, who grows her own hala trees, conducts this family-friendly, hour-long class each week. First, leaves are gathered, dethorned, and wiped clean of dirt and insects. The middle stem is removed with a sharp knife, and the leaf is softened by hand with a dull knife. Then the leaf is cut with a wooden, steel-bladed hand-cutter, which is calibrated depending on the item being created, such as a bracelet, hat, or purse.

THE ST. ANTHONY STEINWAY

The St. Anthony hotel's **Steinway** was built in 1924 for the Russian Embassy in Paris. Featuring a custom-made rosewood case with tulip wood inlay, the piano was assembled in New York, then decorated in France with fine marquetry inlay and gilt bronze mounts. The Russians sold the instrument in 1930 for $27,000, equivalent to $441,000 today, to raise money for the Soviet Union's war debt. The buyer happened to be globe-trotting St. Anthony owner Ralph Morrison, who was searching for treasures for his hotel's museum-like lobby, Peacock Alley. The piano spent almost four decades at home here, being expertly played nightly by San Antonio's finest musicians. It was the linchpin connecting the hotel to the surrounding city. Though it left the St. Anthony in 1993 for the San Francisco home of Larry Chan, owner and chairman of Park Lane Hotels, it was put back on the market in 2013 by fine-arts auction house Bonhams but was no longer in playable condition. Steinway completed a $35,000 repair job before the coveted piece was returned to the hotel, where its beautiful sound and elegance are celebrated once again.

THE WHITLEY

ATLANTA, GEORGIA, USA

A DOGWOOD GROWS
IN BUCKHEAD

Back in the 1800s before Atlanta was a thriving metropolitan hub, Atlanta was a wild and rural land. Through the years, with the help of a settler named John Whitley, the community of Buckhead was established as a gathering place where curious and adventurous souls could trade ideas. Today, Buckhead presents a destination where travelers and locals gather to explore world-class shopping, epicurean delights, exquisite architecture, and notable art galleries. Flowering dogwood trees indigenous to Georgia grow throughout Buckhead, perhaps even marking the spot where John Whitley first planted here. On display in the lounging vignettes at Trade Root Restaurant and Lounge are portraits by **Marian Westall** that depict a man and woman in formal dress with dogwood blossoms placed over their faces. Westall's portraits both hark back to Atlanta's roots and reflect the progressive landscape of The Whitley's surroundings. Symbolizing rebirth in the springtime as well as the rebirth of Buckhead's best new hotel, the dogwood can be found in The Whitley's emblem, art, floral designs, and curated cocktails.

A PRESIDENTIAL PORTRAIT

4212　Grand Stairway, U. S. Grant Hotel, San Diego, Cal.
COPYRIGHT ENO & MATTESON 1910.

The portrait of Civil War general and eighteenth US president Ulysses S. Grant is the pride of the historic art collection located inside THE US GRANT. Ulysses S. Grant, Jr., the president's second son, had visions of building a grand hotel in his father's honor, and on October 15, 1910, that hotel opened its doors. For the occasion, the Grant family commissioned **Urban Lawrence Gray** to paint an oil on canvas. The portrait was originally installed in the lobby at the top of the grand staircase. For the hotel's 2006 reopening, it was carefully restored and displayed in the foyer at the heart of the lower level. Today, it is hung at the entrance and welcomes guests to the hotel in the same fashion as a patriarch or monarch portrait would in a mansion or palace. In 2003, the Sycuan Tribal Development Corporation, the business arm of Sycuan, a sovereign tribe of the Kumeyaay Nation, acquired THE US GRANT for $45 million. The Kumeyaay now carry on the legacy of President Grant, who supported Native American rights and passed an executive order in the 1870s to set aside 640 acres of land in East County for the Kumeyaay. Due in great part to the president's efforts, the US government officially recognized the sovereign status of these California tribes by passing the Mission Indians Relief Act in 1891.

THE LUXURY COLLECTION
HOTEL DIRECTORY

AFRICA

ETHIOPIA
SHERATON ADDIS

From the crystal clear pool with soft underwater music to the yearly Ethiopian art exhibition, the hotel is the perfect place to indulge and experience the culture of Addis Ababa.

Taitu Street, P.O. Box 6002
Addis Ababa
telephone 251 11 517 1717

luxurycollection.com/addis

ASIA

CHINA
THE AZURE QIANTANG

The mythic Qiantang River sets the scene at The Azure Qiantang, where the concierge recommends a private sculling boat trip to explore an ancient pilgrimage route and the largest tidal bore in the world.

39 East Wangjiang Road
Shangcheng District
Hangzhou, Zhejiang 310008
telephone 86 571 2823 7777

luxurycollection.com/azureqiantang

CHINA
THE CASTLE HOTEL

Overlooking vibrant Xinghai Bay, The Castle Hotel boasts three sophisticated restaurants, a lounge, and a spa. Its grand ballrooms serve as settings for truly memorable occasions.

600 Binhai West Road
Shahekou District
Dalian, Liaoning 116023
telephone 86 411 8656 0000

luxurycollection.com/castle

CHINA
THE GRAND MANSION

In the heart of Nanjing's cultural district, this iconic hotel unites the city's fabled past with destination dining and modern amenities.

300 Changjiang Road
Nanjing, Jiangsu 210005
telephone 86 25 8435 5888

luxurycollection.com/grandmansion

CHINA
THE HONGTA HOTEL

Sweeping views of Shanghai, personalized butler service, and the award-winning Italian restaurant Danieli's make one's stay at The Hongta Hotel a first-class experience.

889 Dong Fang Road, Pudong District
Shanghai 200122
telephone 86 21 5050 4567

luxurycollection.com/hongta

CHINA
MEIXI LAKE HOTEL

Elegant accommodations and modern facilities blend into an urban oasis of serene lake views, captivating culture, and layered history.

1177 Huanhu Road, Yuelu District
Changsha, Hunan 410006
telephone 86 731 8869 8888

luxurycollection.com/meixilake

CHINA

TWELVE AT HENGSHAN

Located on the beautiful tree-lined Hengshan Road, this modern, stylish newcomer is a stone's throw from the city's trendy shopping area, restaurants, parks, and museums.

12 Hengshan Road, Xuhui District
Shanghai 200031
telephone 86 21 3338 3888

luxurycollection.com/12hengshan

INDIA

ITC GARDENIA

Set in the commercial heart of Bengaluru, ITC Gardenia is a verdant sanctuary exuding natural sophistication and elegance. Combined with its ambience of nature embracing luxury, warm hospitality, and superlative facilities, ITC Gardenia lives the "Responsible Luxury" promise and is a tribute to the Garden City.

1 Residency Road, Bengaluru
Karnataka 560025
telephone 91 80 2211 9898

luxurycollection.com/itcgardenia

INDIA

ITC GRAND BHARAT

The resort's 300 acres encompass elaborate culinary experiences, conference facilities, and recreation and wellness services. Envisioned as a supreme leisure getaway destination, the hotel is situated in an idyllic expanse, just outside Delhi, surrounded by the majestic Aravalli range and dotted with pristine lakes.

Gurgaon, New Delhi Capital Region
PO: Hasanpur, Dist: Mewat, Haryana 122105
telephone 91 1267 285 500

luxurycollection.com/itcgrandbharat

INDIA

ITC GRAND CENTRAL

The palatial hotel evokes Mumbai's colonial grandeur with authentic décor and worldly amenities. ITC Grand Central represents the patchwork of Mumbai's cultures—its English charm, mercantile past, and modern present—effortlessly blending old and new Bombay.

Dr Babasaheb Ambedkar Road
Parel, Mumbai
Maharashtra 400012
telephone 91 22 2410 1010

luxurycollection.com/itcgrandcentral

INDIA

ITC GRAND CHOLA

In its grandeur and majesty, this 600-room masterpiece is an inspired rendition of the vision of South India's great masters. With a perfect synergy of history, refined opulence, and unparalleled service, guests can enjoy an exceptional indigenous luxury experience.

63 Mount Road, Guindy, Chennai
Tamil Nadu 600032
telephone 91 44 2220 0000

luxurycollection.com/itcgrandchola

INDIA

ITC KAKATIYA

Discover opulence in the heart of Hyderabad's commercial district, as authentic Kakatiya décor unites with singular views of Lake Hussain Sagar. This luxury hotel is a true homage to the legendary Kakatiya Dynasty.

6-3-1187 Begumpet, Hyderabad
Telangana 500016
telephone 91 40 2340 0132

luxurycollection.com/itckakatiya

INDIA
ITC MARATHA

Elegance and history merge to reveal the city's rich culture. Saluting the legacy of the Grand Marathas, this hotel presents a range of cuisines, accommodations, and recreational options with the warmth of Indian hospitality for an unmistakably majestic experience.

Sahar Airport Road, Near International Airport
Mumbai, Maharashtra 400099
telephone 91 22 2830 3030

luxurycollection.com/itcmaratha

INDIA
ITC MAURYA

Situated in the diplomatic enclave of New Delhi, with more than 400 luxurious rooms and suites, in addition to world-renowned cuisine and a deep understanding of the needs of the global traveler, this hotel is the preferred accommodation for heads of state, royalty, and business leaders.

Diplomatic Enclave
New Delhi 110021
telephone 91 11 2611 2233

luxurycollection.com/itcmaurya

INDIA
ITC MUGHAL

Sprawled over 35 acres of lush gardens and water features near the magnificent Taj Mahal, this hotel is a tribute to the Mughal era. ITC Mughal boasts the country's largest and most luxurious spa, Kaya Kalp–the Royal Spa, along with a range of fine-dining options.

Taj Ganj, Agra
Uttar Pradesh 282001
telephone 91 562 402 1700

luxurycollection.com/itcmughal

INDIA
ITC RAJPUTANA

Centrally located, ITC Rajputana is the perfect blend of Rajasthani architecture and Rajput hospitality. The *haveli*-inspired architecture and regal design echo the city's history, while the balconies from the guest rooms face an intricate network of internal courtyards.

Palace Road, Jaipur
Rajasthan 302006
telephone 91 141 510 0100

luxurycollection.com/itcrajputana

INDIA
ITC SONAR

Celebrating the Golden Era of Bengal, ITC Sonar is a verdant oasis just minutes from the heart of Kolkata. Garden houses, large green spaces, and water features reminiscent of the Baghbaris create a captivating setting, while a well-appointed spa provides modern-day comforts in the City of Joy.

JBS Haldane Avenue, Kolkata
West Bengal 700046
telephone 91 33 2345 4545

luxurycollection.com/itcsonar

INDIA
ITC WINDSOR

ITC Windsor's elegant colonnades, fluted pillars, Georgian windows, and magnificent chandeliers create a stirring ambience of old-world leisure. Experience the glory of the days of the Raj, minutes from downtown Bengaluru, where the colonial past meets modern luxury.

Windsor Square, 25, Golf Course Road
Bangaluru, Karnataka 560052
telephone 91 80 2226 9898

luxurycollection.com/itcwindsor

INDONESIA
KERATON AT THE PLAZA

This beautiful hotel celebrates the richness of Indonesian culture and local Javanese traditions through its art gallery and cuisine.

Jl. MH. Thamrin Kav. 15
Jakarta 10350
telephone 62 21 5068 0000

luxurycollection.com/keraton

INDONESIA
THE LAGUNA

Nestled on Bali's finest white-sand beach overlooking the majestic Indian Ocean and infinite swimmable lagoons, The Laguna is situated perfectly in the enchanting Nusa Dua enclave.

Kawasan Pariwisata Nusa Dua Lot N2
Nusa Dua, Bali 80363
telephone 62 361 771327

luxurycollection.com/bali

JAPAN
THE PRINCE GALLERY TOKYO KIOICHO

Near businesses and landmarks in Tokyo's most dignified neighborhood, guests are welcomed in innovative interiors and upscale guest rooms.

1-2 Kioi-cho Chiyoda-ku, Tokyo
telephone 81 3 3234 1111

luxurycollection.com/princegallery

JAPAN
SUIRAN

This hotel offers authentic Japanese experiences within a historic Kyoto community—a peaceful riverfront haven steps from the Tenryu-ji, World Heritage Site.

Saga-Tenryuji, Ukyo-Ku
12 Susukinobaba-Cho
Kyoto
telephone 81 75 872 0101

luxurycollection.com/suiran

MALAYSIA
THE ANDAMAN

Stunning sunsets, crystal blue waters, rainforest trails, and coral reef walks are just some of the extraordinary experiences this hotel offers guests.

Jalan Teluk Datai
Langkawi, 07000
telephone 60 4 959 1088

luxurycollection.com/andaman

THAILAND
THE ATHENEE HOTEL

Located on the grounds of Kandhavas Palace, this iconic hotel is renowned as one of the most prestigious addresses in central Bangkok.

61 Wireless Road (Witthayu)
Lumpini, Pathumwan
Bangkok 10330
telephone 66 26 508 800

luxurycollection.com/theatheneehotel

THAILAND
THE NAKA ISLAND

With endless views of Phang Nga Bay and the Phuket landscape, this five-star island retreat is private, romantic, and idyllic.

32 Moo 5, Tambol Paklok
Amphur Thalang, Naka Yai Island
Phuket 83110
telephone 66 76 371 400

luxurycollection.com/nakaisland

THAILAND
SHERATON GRANDE SUKHUMVIT

This hotel is home to Basil, one of the finest Thai restaurants in Bangkok, where chef Kesinee Wanta crafts creative dishes with the exquisite flavors from every culinary region of Thailand.

250 Sukhumvit Road
Bangkok 10110
telephone 66 2 649 8888

luxurycollection.com/grandesukhumvit

THAILAND
VANA BELLE

Poised overlooking the breathtaking Gulf of Siam, Vana Belle offers an enchanting getaway and memorable experiences in one of Thailand's most beautiful locations.

9/99 Moo 3, Chaweng Noi Beach, Surat Thani
Koh Samui 84320
telephone 66 77 915 555

luxurycollection.com/vanabellesamui

EUROPE

ARMENIA
THE ALEXANDER

The mixture of old and new is exemplified by The Alexander, which boasts a prestigious central location one block from Charles Aznavour Square.

3/4 Abovyan Street
Yerevan 0001
telephone 374 1 120 6000

luxurycollection.com/alexander

AUSTRIA
HOTEL BRISTOL

Located near the Vienna State Opera in the heart of the city, this luxury hotel provides an oasis from the bustle of a busy metropolis. The concierge recommends visiting the elegant Winter Palace of Prince Eugene of Savoy, right in the city center.

Kaerntner Ring 1
Vienna 1010
telephone 43 1 515 160

luxurycollection.com/bristol

AUSTRIA
HOTEL GOLDENER HIRSCH

Sip the signature Susanne cocktail, eat the famous Rigo Jancsi dessert, and live in luxury while attending nearby summer festivals in Salzburg.

Getreidegasse 37
Salzburg 5020
telephone 43 6 628 0840

luxurycollection.com/goldenerhirsch

AUSTRIA
HOTEL IMPERIAL

Experience the essence of Vienna at this elegant and beautiful hotel and delight in the Viennese coffee tradition by enjoying a cup of Imperial coffee and a slice of the renowned torte.

Kaerntner Ring 16
Vienna, 1015
telephone 43 1 501 100

luxurycollection.com/imperial

AUSTRIA
SCHLOSS FUSCHL

Enjoy a valuable collection of Old Masters, a lush golf course, and fresh fish from the castle fishery at this hotel.

Schloss Strasse 19
Hof bei Salzburg 5322
telephone 43 6 229 22530

luxurycollection.com/schlossfuschl

BULGARIA
SOFIA HOTEL BALKAN

Located in downtown Sofia, this luxury hotel offers an exceptional experience of Bulgaria's finest culture and service.

5 Sveta Nedelya Square
Sofia 1000
telephone 359 2 981 6541

luxurycollection.com/sofia

CYPRUS
PARKLANE

Surrounded by landscaped gardens, the resort welcomes guests with a picturesque lane that snakes through a verdant grove of evergreen olive, citrus, and palm trees.

11 Giannou Kranidioti Street
Limassol 4534
telephone 357 25 862000

CZECH REPUBLIC
AUGUSTINE

Located in a thirteenth-century Augustinian monastery, the hotel boasts impeccable service and design inspired by early-twentieth-century Czech cubism.

Letenská 12/33
Prague 118 00
telephone 420 2 6611 2233

luxurycollection.com/augustine

FRANCE
HOTEL DE BERRI

Located in the fashionable eighth arrondissement, the hotel is distinguished by an expansive private park and an extraordinary art collection.

18–22 Rue de Berri
Paris, 75008
telephone 33 1 76 53 77 70

luxurycollection.com/hoteldeberri

FRANCE
PRINCE DE GALLES

Just steps away from the Champs-Élysées, this Art Deco hotel, a mosaic of discrete Parisian elegance, is located in the heart of the city and offers exceptional hospitality and superb cuisine by culinary talent Stéphanie Le Quellec.

33 Avenue George V
Paris 75008
telephone 33 1 53 237777

luxurycollection.com/princedegalles

GERMANY
HOTEL FUERSTENHOF

Relax in the AquaMarin spa, the landscaped pool, the Finnish sauna, or the Roman steam bath and restore harmony to your body at this luxury hotel.

Troendlinring 8
Leipzig 04105
telephone 49 341 1400

luxurycollection.com/fuerstenhof

GREECE
BLUE PALACE

Discover beauty in this hotel's emblematic views, tranquility at its Elounda Spa on the beach, and fun at the nearby Crete Golf Club.

P.O. Box 38
Elounda, Crete 72053
telephone 30 284 106 5500

luxurycollection.com/bluepalace

GREECE
HOTEL GRANDE BRETAGNE

With unsurpassed views of the Acropolis and Parthenon, Constitution Square, and Lycabettus Hill, this hotel offers unrivaled access to Athens's mythical history.

Vas Georgiou A' Street 1
Athens 10564
telephone 30 210 333 0000

luxurycollection.com/grandebretagne

GREECE
KING GEORGE

Just two kilometers from the Acropolis, this hotel has welcomed many celebrities and hosted many events in its 350-square-meter room under the illuminated sky.

Vas Georgiou A' Street 3
Athens 10564
telephone 30 210 322 2210

luxurycollection.com/kinggeorge

GREECE
MYSTIQUE

Guests can visit the Secret Wine Cave, take in the beauty of the surrounding views, and restore at the spa while visiting this luxury resort.

Oia
Santorini Island
Santorini, South Aegean 84702
telephone 30 228 607 1114

luxurycollection.com/mystique

GREECE
THE ROMANOS

Guests can indulge in one of Anazoe Spa's signature treatments, experience tours from Navarino Outdoors, and scuba dive with Navarino Sea—all experiences that can be arranged by the concierge.

Navarino Dunes, Messinia
Costa Navarino 24001
telephone 30 272 309 6000

luxurycollection.com/theromanos

GREECE
SANTA MARINA

A paradise within a paradise, this hotel is a tranquil oasis where one can indulge in spa treatments and fine dining surrounded by the natural beauty of Mykonos.

Ornos Bay
Mykonos, South Aegean 84600
telephone 30 228 902 3220

luxurycollection.com/santamarina

GREECE
VEDEMA

Surrounded by historical sites, beautiful beaches, and hot springs, this luxury resort has plenty to explore.

Megalohori
Santorini, South Aegean 84700
telephone 30 228 608 1796

luxurycollection.com/vedema

ITALY
CRISTALLO

Complete relaxation, elegant cuisine, and natural beauty await guests of this resort's refined facilities and fin de siècle atmosphere.

Via Rinaldo Menardi 42
Cortina d'Ampezzo 32043
telephone 39 043 688 1111

luxurycollection.com/cristallo

ITALY
EXCELSIOR HOTEL GALLIA

Located at the heart of fashion capital Milan, Excelsior Hotel Gallia provides the ideal setting for sophistication. The concierge suggests an evening at the world-renowned La Scala Opera House.

Piazza Duca D'Aosta 9
Milan 20124
telephone 39 02 67851

luxurycollection.com/excelsiorgallia

ITALY
FALISIA

Indulge in delectable multicultural cuisine and indelible experiences in and along the Gulf of Trieste.

Località Sistiana 231/M
Portopiccolo 34011
telephone 39 040 997 4444

luxurycollection.com/falisia

ITALY
THE GRITTI PALACE

Occupying a prestigious setting on the Grand Canal, The Gritti Palace recently reopened after a meticulous restoration. A leisurely short stroll from Piazza San Marco, the imposing palazzo awards rare views of Santa Maria della Salute.

Campo Santa Maria del Giglio
Venice 30124
telephone 39 0417 94611

luxurycollection.com/grittipalace

ITALY
HOTEL CALA DI VOLPE

Horseback riding, tennis, and golf are just some of the fun outdoor activities to enjoy at this hotel.

Costa Smeralda
Porto Cervo 07020
telephone 39 0789 976111

luxurycollection.com/caladivolpe

ITALY
HOTEL DANIELI

Located within walking distance of Saint Mark's Square, this legendary hotel allows visitors to shop, dine, and experience Venice to the fullest.

Castello 4196
Venice 30122
telephone 39 041 522 6480

luxurycollection.com/danieli

ITALY
HOTEL PITRIZZA

Experience local traditions and cuisine firsthand with the hotel's full immersion opportunities, including local artisan demonstrations.

Costa Smeralda
Porto Cervo 07020
telephone 39 0789 930111

luxurycollection.com/hotelpitrizza

ITALY
HOTEL ROMAZZINO

Enjoy local food and activities such as horseback riding and sailing at this beautiful resort.

Costa Smeralda
Porto Cervo 07020
telephone 39 0789 977111

luxurycollection.com/romazzino

THE NETHERLANDS
HOTEL DES INDES

This luxury hotel is located in the heart of The Hague and is an ideal starting point for exploring local attractions such as the Royal Picture Gallery Mauritshuis and the antique market.

Lange Voorhout 54–56
The Hague 2514 EG
telephone 31 70 361 2345

luxurycollection.com/desindes

POLAND
HOTEL BRISTOL

This hotel lies right on the Royal Route, a road that leads through the historic district of the city and is dotted with examples of stunning architecture from the sixteenth century to the present day.

Krakowskie Przedmiescie 42/44
Warsaw 00-325
telephone 48 22 551 1000

luxurycollection.com/bristolwarsaw

PORTUGAL
PINE CLIFFS

Enjoy breathtaking views of the surroundings, warm weather year-round, and the beautiful golf course, including its famed and most challenging golf hole, Devil's Parlour, at this luxury hotel.

Praia de Falesia, Apartado P.O. Box 644
Algarve 8200
telephone 351 289 500100

luxurycollection.com/algarve

RUSSIA
HOTEL NATIONAL

Exploring Moscow was never easier, as this hotel offers spectacular views of the Kremlin and Red Square, while being only steps away from attractions such as the Bolshoi Theatre.

15/1 Mokhovaya Street
Moscow 125009
telephone 7 495 258 7000

luxurycollection.com/national

SERBIA
METROPOL PALACE

This hotel has always been the heart of Belgrade's social life and is an indelible landmark in the city skyline, overlooking Tasmajdan Park.

Bulevar Kralja Aleksandra 69
Belgrade 11000
telephone 381 11 333 3100

luxurycollection.com/metropolpalace

SLOVAKIA
GRAND HOTEL RIVER PARK

The Slovakian capital's leading hotel is distinguished by its accessibility, sleek décor, spacious accommodations, and expansive spa.

Dvorakovo Nabrezie 6
Bratislava 81102
telephone 421 2 32238 222

luxurycollection.com/grandhotelriverpark

SPAIN
CASTILLO HOTEL SON VIDA

A first-class beauty spa, breathtaking golf courses, and a Kids' Club equipped with a separate pool area and playground are all offered at this hotel.

C/Raixa 2, Urbanizacion Son Vida
Mallorca 07013
telephone 34 971 493493

luxurycollection.com/castillo

SPAIN
HOTEL ALFONSO XIII

This hotel is one of the most monumental landmarks in Seville, embodying the city's layered history, architecture, and authentic cuisine in a luxurious atmosphere.

San Fernando 2
Seville 41004
telephone 34 95 491 7000

luxurycollection.com/hotelalfonso

SPAIN
HOTEL MARIA CRISTINA

Indulge in a mouthwatering local culinary experience when visiting this charming hotel, near the Michelin-starred restaurants of San Sebastián.

Paseo Republica Argentina 4
San Sebastián 20004
telephone 34 943 437600

luxurycollection.com/mariacristina

SPAIN
HOTEL MARQUÉS DE RISCAL

Frank Gehry's design houses a collection of wines that any wine lover will enjoy. The hotel offers guided cultural tours to truly take in the surrounding area.

Calle Torrea 1
Elciego 01340
telephone 34 945 180880

luxurycollection.com/marquesderiscal

SWITZERLAND
HOTEL PRESIDENT WILSON

Located minutes away from Geneva's lakefront, this luxury hotel allows one to explore such local attractions as the Jet d'Eau, Flower Clock, and St. Peter's Cathedral.

47, Quai Wilson
Geneva 1211
telephone 41 22 906 6666

luxurycollection.com/presidentwilson

TURKEY
CARESSE

Truly indulgent ESPA treatments, a picnic on a private yacht, breathtaking views from relaxing accommodations—all are possible here.

Adnan Menderes caddesi No. 89
Asarlik Mevkii PK 225
Bodrum 48400

telephone 90 252 311 3636

luxurycollection.com/caresse

TURKEY
LUGAL

Immerse yourself in local culture, as original paintings by local artists are found throughout this luxury hotel.

Noktali Sokak No. 1, 'Kavaklidere
Ankara 06700
telephone 90 312 457 6050

luxurycollection.com/lugal

UNITED KINGDOM
THE PARK TOWER KNIGHTSBRIDGE

While at this hotel, guests can visit the vibrant Serpentine Gallery, and dine at One-O-One, which is under the auspices of acclaimed chef Pascal Proyart and is recognized as the city's best fish restaurant by critics and locals alike.

101 Knightsbridge
London, Great Britain SW1X 7RN
telephone 44 207 235 8050

luxurycollection.com/parktowerlondon

UNITED KINGDOM
TRUMP TURNBERRY

From world-class golfing facilities, including the nine-hole Arran course, to quad biking and horseback riding, to private tours of the magnificent surrounding areas, which can be arranged by the concierge, this luxury hotel is an outdoorsman's sanctuary.

Turnberry Ayrshire KA26 9LT
Scotland
telephone 44 165 533 1000

luxurycollection.com/trumpturnberry

UNITED KINGDOM
THE WELLESLEY KNIGHTSBRIDGE

Boutique and grand elements exist harmoniously in this Knightsbridge hotel near fabled parks, renowned shopping, and historic landmarks.

11 Knightsbridge
London, Great Britain SW1X 7LY
telephone 44 20 7235 3535

luxurycollection.com/
wellesleyknightsbridge

UNITED KINGDOM
THE WESTBURY MAYFAIR

Thoughtfully redesigned accommodations and elegant facilities distinguish this hotel in Mayfair, near renowned fashion destinations.

37 Conduit Street
London, Great Britain W1S 2YF
telephone 44 207 629 7755

luxurycollection.com/westbury

LATIN AMERICA

ARGENTINA
PARK TOWER

Unparalleled service, an in-hotel shopping arcade, and a heart-of-the-city location set this luxury hotel apart.

Avenida Leandro N. Alem 1193
Buenos Aires 1001
telephone 54 11 4318 9100

luxurycollection.com/parktower

CHILE
SAN CRISTOBAL TOWER

A bicycle tour of the bohemian Bellavista neighborhood, picnics at the nearby Concha y Toro Vineyard, and skiing on the best slopes in South America are all offered at this luxury hotel.

Josefina Edwards de Ferrari 0100
Santiago
telephone 56 2 2707 1000

luxurycollection.com/sancristobaltower

MEXICO
HACIENDA PUERTA CAMPECHE

This hotel is a collection of restored seventeenth-century historical houses, allowing one to enjoy the beauty of a Mexican hacienda with excellent personal service.

Calle 59, No. 71 por 16 & 18
Campeche, Campeche 24000
telephone 52 981 816 7508

luxurycollection.com/puertacampeche

MEXICO
HACIENDA SAN JOSE

An authentic Mayan experience can be had in the Mayan Villas, while luxury can be found through massages in the privacy of the spa area.

KM 30 Carretera Tixkokob-Tekanto
Tixkokob, Yucatán 97470
telephone 52 999 924 1333

luxurycollection.com/sanjose

MEXICO
HACIENDA SANTA ROSA

Bird watching, Mayan lessons, cocktail demonstrations, and tours of the botanical garden are all offered at this luxury hotel.

KM 129 Carretera Merida Campeche
Santa Rosa, Yucatán 97800
telephone 52 999 923 1923

luxurycollection.com/santarosa

MEXICO
HACIENDA TEMOZON

Explore the unique Hol Be Spa, where one can experience individual spa treatments in a beautifully preserved cavern.

KM 182 Carretera Merida-Uxmal
Temozon Sur, Yucatán 97825
telephone 52 999 923 8089

luxurycollection.com/temozon

MEXICO
HACIENDA UAYAMON

Bulbous pegs set into stone walls can be found throughout this hotel, allowing guests to hang woven cotton hammocks and sleep in the Mayan style.

KM 20 Carretera Uayamon-China-Edzná
Uayamon, Campeche
telephone 52 981 813 0530

luxurycollection.com/uayamon

MEXICO
LAS ALCOBAS

Refined hospitality and unforgettable wellbeing and culinary experiences await in this hotel's artistic fusion of modernity, elegance, and comfort.

Ave. Presidente Masaryk 390
Mexico City, Federal District 11560
telephone 52 55 3300 3900

luxurycollection.com/
lasalcobasmexicocity

MEXICO
SOLAZ

Discover Solaz's striking architecture, which seamlessly blends the destination's unique landscape where the desert meets the sea.

KM 18.5 Carretera Transpeninsular CSL-SJC
Cabo Real, San Jose del Cabo
Baja California Sur 23405
telephone 52 624 144 0500

luxurycollection.com/solaz

PANAMA
THE SANTA MARIA

In the heart of Panama, this contemporary hotel invites guests to uncover the cobblestone streets of Panama Viejo and modern marvels like Frank Gehry's Biomuseo.

Santa Maria Boulevard
Panama City
telephone 507 304 5555

luxurycollection.com/santamaria

PERU
PALACIO DEL INKA

Located in the historic center of Cusco, this hotel dates back almost five centuries and offers easy access to museums, markets, and restaurants. Its property also boasts a relaxing therapy pool.

Plazoleta Santo Domingo 259
Cusco
telephone 51 84 231 961

luxurycollection.com/palaciodelinka

PERU
HOTEL PARACAS

A bottle of local pisco, wind-surfing lessons, and private-jet flights over the Nazca Lines are all offered at this luxury hotel. The concierge suggests traveling back in time with a visit to the intriguing archaeological site Tambo Colorado.

Av. Paracas S/N
Paracas
telephone 51 56 581 333

luxurycollection.com/hotelparacas

PERU
TAMBO DEL INKA

Enjoy views of the Vilcanota River while swimming in the hotel pool. Take a guided trip to the Valle Sagrado and escape to Machu Picchu from the hotel's private train station.

Avenida Ferrocarril S/N
Sacred Valley, Urubamba
telephone 51 84 581 777

luxurycollection.com/tambodelinka

MIDDLE EAST

KUWAIT
SHERATON KUWAIT

Situated in the middle of Kuwait's commercial center, the hotel boasts a health club that offers a variety of revitalizing, relaxing, and pampering treatments.

Safat 13060 / Fahd Al-Salem Street
P.O. Box 5902 Safat
Kuwait City 13060
telephone 965 2242 2055

luxurycollection.com/kuwait

JORDAN
AL MANARA

Jordan's rich culture is reflected in the traditional architecture, sumptuous decor, and magnificent surroundings of this seaside escape.

King Hussein Street
Saraya Aqaba
Aqaba 77110
telephone 962 3202 1000

luxurycollection.com/almanara

LEBANON
GRAND HILLS

Lush greenery and pine forests carpet the locale of Grand Hills, and the nearby Beirut coast offers amazing Mediterranean views. For the more adventurous, the concierge suggests traveling up the coast to Byblos, the world's oldest continually inhabited city.

Charkieh Main Road
Broumana 1204
telephone 961 4 868 888

luxurycollection.com/grandhills

U.A.E.
AJMAN SARAY

Situated along the Arabian Gulf, just minutes from Dubai, this resort overlooks endless expanses of pristine sand and shimmering sea.

Sheikh Humaid Bin Rashid Al Nuaimi Street
Ajman 8833
telephone 971 6 714 2222

luxurycollection.com/ajmansaray

U.A.E.
AL MAHA

Arabian wildlife—with Arabian oryx and gazelles as the star attractions—can be seen from the temperature-controlled infinity pools or sundeck areas of all villas.

Dubai–Al Ain Road
Dubai
telephone 971 4 832 9900

luxurycollection.com/almaha

U.A.E.
GROSVENOR HOUSE

This lifestyle destination, located in the cosmopolitan area of Dubai Marina, offers access to fantastic restaurants, including the hotel's world-famous Buddha Bar.

Al Emreef Street
P.O. Box 118500
Dubai
telephone 971 4 399 8888

luxurycollection.com/grosvenorhouse

NORTH AMERICA

UNITED STATES
THE BALLANTYNE

Located on a championship PGA golf course, this Southern beauty features signature cocktails, luxurious lodging, and spa treatments.

10000 Ballantyne Commons Parkway
Charlotte, North Carolina 28277
telephone 1 704 248 4000

luxurycollection.com/ballantyne

UNITED STATES
THE CANYON SUITES AT THE PHOENICIAN

Discover Arizona's only Forbes Five-Star, AAA Five Diamond resort. Enjoy complimentary daily wine tastings, chauffeured resort and local transportation, and a private infinity pool.

6000 East Camelback Road
Scottsdale, Arizona 85251
telephone 1 480 941 8200

luxurycollection.com/canyonsuites

UNITED STATES
THE CHATWAL
This Stanford White landmark was once home to the famed Lambs Club and now offers guests the same glamorous treatment with luxurious accommodations and striking Art Deco interior design.

130 West 44th Street
New York, New York 10036
telephone 1 212 764 6200

luxurycollection.com/chatwal

UNITED STATES
THE EQUINOX
With beautiful mountain views, a world-class spa, and suites with fireplaces, enjoy cozy days and nights at this Vermont treasure.

3567 Main Street
Manchester Village, Vermont 05254
telephone 1 802 362 4700

luxurycollection.com/equinox

UNITED STATES
THE GWEN
This opulent hotel along the Magnificent Mile boasts modern amenities, spacious guest rooms, and fine dining in an inviting atmosphere.

521 North Rush Street
Chicago, Illinois 60611
telephone 1 312 645 1500

luxurycollection.com/thegwen

UNITED STATES
HOTEL IVY
Of all the destinations to be discovered, few are filled with such surprises as the contemporary yet affable Minneapolis. The Hotel Ivy is the key to unlocking your guide to indigenous, exceptional, and collectible experiences.

201 South Eleventh Street
Minneapolis, Minnesota 55403
telephone 1 612 746 4600

luxurycollection.com/ivy

UNITED STATES
HOTEL TALISA
Tucked into protected forestland at the base of Vail Mountain amid soaring evergreens and aspen, Hotel Talisa promises four seasons of alpine beauty and activity.

1300 Westhaven Drive
Vail, Colorado 81657
telephone 1 970 476 7111

UNITED STATES
LAS ALCOBAS
With premier spa and dining facilities, this inspiring St. Helena hotel refines the art of hospitality in California's iconic Wine Country.

1915 Main Street
St. Helena, California 94574
telephone 707 963 7000

luxurycollection.com/lasalcobas

UNITED STATES
THE LIBERTY
Guests of the beautiful hotel are exposed to the best of Boston, from sweeping views of the skyline to complimentary Liberty-branded bicycles for riding around town. The iconic Freedom Trail is a must for any history buff.

215 Charles Street
Boston, Massachusetts 02114
telephone 1 617 224 4000

luxurycollection.com/libertyhotel

UNITED STATES
THE NINES
Known for its creative and unique personal service, this hotel offers guests a customized nightly turn-down, and a seasonal and tasty snack.

525 SW Morrison Street
Portland, Oregon 97204
telephone 1 877 229 9995

luxurycollection.com/thenines

UNITED STATES
PALACE HOTEL
Commanding its location in the heart of vibrant San Francisco, this hotel provides guests with hospitality on a grand scale.

2 New Montgomery Street
San Francisco, California 94105
telephone 1 415 512 1111

luxurycollection.com/palacehotel

UNITED STATES
PERRY LANE HOTEL
Equidistant from River Street and Forsyth Park, this vibrant luxury hotel welcomes guests with worldly elegance and Southern hospitality.

256 East Perry Street
Savannah, Georgia 31401
telephone 1 912 415 9000

luxurycollection.com/perrylane

UNITED STATES
THE PHOENICIAN
Nestled at the base of Camelback Mountain, golfing, swimming, tennis, and first-class spa treatments are some of the activities guests can enjoy at this awe-inspiring Sonoran destination.

6000 East Camelback Road
Scottsdale, Arizona 85251
telephone 1 480 941 8200

luxurycollection.com/phoenician

UNITED STATES
THE ROYAL HAWAIIAN
Offering Hawaiian hospitality since 1927, the iconic "Pink Palace of the Pacific" graces the perfect location on Waikiki Beach. The hotel combines historical legacy with contemporary comfort for the discerning world traveler seeking an idyllic location in paradise.

2259 Kalakaua Avenue
Honolulu, Hawaii 96815
telephone 1 808 923 7311

luxurycollection.com/royalhawaiian

UNITED STATES
SLS HOTEL
Designed by Philippe Starck, the hotel challenges every traditional convention of luxury hospitality, from a culinary program crafted by Spanish chef José Andrés to a unique spa concept at Ciel Spa.

465 S. La Cienega Boulevard
Los Angeles, California 90048
telephone 1 310 247 0400

luxurycollection.com/sls

UNITED STATES
THE ST. ANTHONY
Located in the heart of historic San Antonio, and in walking distance of the famed River Walk, this national landmark hotel features first-class amenities including the Peacock Alley Bar, where guests can enjoy a cocktail in the plush leather chairs next to the fireplace.

300 East Travis Street
San Antonio, Texas 78205
telephone 1 210 227 4392

luxurycollection.com/stanthony

UNITED STATES
THE US GRANT
A presidential landmark nestled amid the vibrancy of downtown San Diego's famed Gaslamp Quarter, the hotel weaves its storied history into an oasis of fine art and epicurean innovation—including The US Grant's 100-day barrel-aged Centennial Manhattan.

326 Broadway
San Diego, California 92101
telephone 1 619 232 3121

luxurycollection.com/usgrant

UNITED STATES
THE WHITLEY
Amid Buckhead's upscale shopping, dining, and nightlife, the hotel's elegance extends from its guest rooms to the spa to ample event space.

3434 Peachtree Road, Northeast
Atlanta, Georgia 30326
telephone 1 404 237 2700

luxurycollection.com/whitley

WHITNEY ROBINSON

Whitney Robinson was named editor in chief of *Elle Decor* in July 2017. Before that, he was style director at *Town & Country*, where he assigned, edited, wrote, and produced style and interiors stories and collaborated on a wide range of topics throughout the magazine. Robinson was deputy editor of the reimagined *Metropolitan Home*, and before that, he was a senior editor at *Town & Country*. He was also the cofounder of Qulture.com, a bilingual digital destination for arts and culture in the Middle East. Robinson has written about interior design, fashion, jewelry, food, and travel for publications including *T: The New York Times Style Magazine*, *WSJ. Magazine*, and *Departures*. He began his career at *House Beautiful*.

ACKNOWLEDGMENTS

The publisher would like to thank Cheryl Della Pietra and Barbara Gogan.

CREDITS